THE
ROTTEN
ROMANS

TERRY DEARY

Illustrated by
Martin Brown

**With thanks to Helen James for her research.
Sine qua non**

Scholastic Children's Books,
Commonwealth House, 1-19 New Oxford Street
London WC1A 1NU, UK

A division of Scholastic Ltd
London ~ New York ~ Toronto ~ Sydney ~ Auckland
Mexico City ~ New Delhi ~ Hong Kong

Published in the UK by Scholastic Ltd, 1994

Text copyright © Terry Deary, 1994
Illustrations copyright © Martin Brown, 1994

ISBN 0 590 55467 0

All rights reserved
Typeset by Goodfellow & Egan Ltd, Cambridge
Printed and bound in Denmark by
Nørhaven Paperback, Viborg

41 43 45 47 49 50 48 46 44 42 40

The right Terry Deary and Martin Brown to be identified as
the suthor and illustrator of this work respectively has been asserted by
them in accordance with the Copyright, Designs and Patents Act, 1988.

Contents

THE ROTTEN ROMANS

Introduction

History can be horrible. Horribly hard to learn. The trouble is it keeps on *changing*. In maths, two and two is *usually* four – and in science water is *always* made up of hydrogen and oxygen.

But in history things aren't that simple. In history a "fact" is sometimes not a fact at all. Really it's just someone's "opinion". And opinions can be different for different people.

For example . . . you probably think your teacher is more horrible than the cold cabbage and custard you had for school dinner. That's *your* opinion. But teacher's mum probably thinks he's sweeter than tea with six sugars. That's *her* opinion.

You could both be right – or both be wrong . . .

See what I mean? Both right, both wrong!

Of course, honest answers like these don't get you gold stars. No! Teachers will try to tell you there are "right" and "wrong" answers even if there aren't.

There are worse things than horrible history. Want to know what? Teachers' jokes are more horrible than the Tower of London Torture Chamber . . .

So, history can be horrible. But when you find the real truth about the past you can suddenly discover it's horribly fascinating. Everyone loves a good murder story – history is full of them, like the murder of Julius Caesar. Blood all over the place.

And there are war stories, thrillers, horror stories and comedies. That's the sort of history you'll find in this book. With a bit of luck you might even horrify your teacher!

TERRIBLE TIMELINES

The rotten Romans' timeline

BC

753   Roman *legend* says Rome was founded by Romulus. The *truth* is that the early Romans were farmers living in a region called Latium.

509   The Romans are fed up with their cruel king, Tarquin. They throw him out and rule themselves (that's called a Republic).

264   First of the Punic Wars against the great enemy, Carthage (in North Africa). Result: Rome 1 Carthage 0.

218   Hannibal of Carthage attacks Rome with the help of elephants. He can't capture Rome but rampages round Italy terrorising people.

202   Scipio takes charge of the Roman Army and beats Hannibal. Rome 2 Carthage 0. The Roman farmers take over more and more land till they have the whole of Italy.

146 Third War to wipe Carthage out forever. Game, set and match to Rome! The Romans get to like the idea of conquering people! They start on the rest of the world.

130 By now the Romans have conquered Greece and most of Spain.

100 Julius Caesar is born.

59 Julius Caesar becomes Consul for the first time.

55 Julius Caesar invades Britain for the first time because (he says) **a)** the Belgae of south Britain are helping the Gauls of north France to rebel against the Romans, and **b)** there is a wealth of tin, copper and lead to be found in Britain.

44 Julius Caesar is elected dictator for life – then murdered!

AD

43 Claudius gives orders for the invasion of Britain . . . again!

60 One tribe, the Iceni, rebel. Queen Boudicca leads them in massacres of Romans. Roman

General Paulinus defeats her and she poisons herself.

80 Julius Agricola completes the invasion (except for the Picts in Scotland).

84 Agricola beats the Picts at Mons Graupius in Scotland.

122 Hadrian starts building a wall across northern England to keep out the Picts.

235–285 Fifty-year period with over 20 Roman emperors – mainly because they keep getting murdered.

313 Emperor Constantine allows Christian worship.

380 Christianity becomes official religion of Rome.

401 Roman troops are being withdrawn from Britain to defend Rome.

410 Barbarian tribes from Germany begin attacks on the empire and Rome itself.

476 The last Roman emperor of the western empire is forced to retire.

1453 The empire of the east falls to the Turks. End of the Roman Empire.

The battling Britons' timeline

BC

6500   The Ice Age ends, the sea level rises. The north-west corner of Europe is cut off by the sea. The British Isles are formed. The islanders are Britons.
3600   The Britons build Stonehenge.
2150   Tin is discovered in the south-west. Mixed with copper it makes the hardest metal yet known to humans – bronze.
900   Britons make human and animal sacrifices at Peterborough.
600   Iron takes over from bronze for making weapons and tools.
70   Druids are becoming powerful leaders of the Britons.
55   Julius Caesar invades but doesn't stay for long.

AD

10   Britain independent from Rome but some British leaders like to copy Roman way of life.

30 The rich south-east of Britain under one ruler – Cunobelinus – who gives himself the Roman name of "Rex", meaning "King".

41 Cunobelinus dies; his sons Togodumnus and Caratacus take over. They're not so keen on the Romans.

42 Verica (king of the Atribates in southern England) is thrown out by his people because he is friendly with Rome. (Caratacus was stirring them up!) Verica flees to Rome and asks for Roman help.

43 The Romans invade and Togodomnus is killed after a battle at the River Medway.

51 After years of resistance Caratacus is betrayed and handed over to the Romans in chains.

60 Queen of the Iceni in East Anglia, Boudicca, leads a rebellion against the Romans and is defeated. The Romans also destroy the Druid sanctuary in Anglesey.

122 Emperor Hadrian's wall is begun, to stop the Picts and Scots invading England.

11

125 Britons are encouraged to join the Roman Army – and become Roman citizens when they retire.

213 *All* free Britons become Roman citizens – but Roman citizens pay Roman taxes!

367 As the Roman Empire weakens, the attacks on Hadrian's Wall increase.

405 As the Romans leave, their way of life leaves soon after – Roman coins are replaced by the ancient custom of bartering.

410 The Emperor Honorius tells the Britons, "Defend yourselves," as the Irish, the Picts, the Scots and the Saxons (from north Germany) begin to raid Britain.

420 Saxons begin to settle in eastern Britain.

443 Plagues in the towns help drive people back to the old British ways of country living.

446 The British appeal to Rome for help against the Saxons. No help arrives. The days of Roman Britain are over. The Saxons have the rich south-east. The Britons have to make do with the poor, wild north and west.

21 Terrible Tribes

KEY

1 DAMNONII	6 PARISI	11 DEMETAE	16 ATREBATES
2 VOTADINI	7 ORDOVICES	12 DOBUNNI	17 BELGAE
3 SELGOVAE	8 CORNOVII	13 CATUVELLAUNI	18 CANTIACI
4 NOVANTAE	9 CORITANI	14 TRINOVANTES	19 REGNENSES
5 BRIGANTES	10 ICENI	15 SILURES	20 DUROTRIGES
			21 DUMNONII

THE ROTTEN ROMAN ARMY

The Roman Army didn't run all of Roman Britain. Once they'd won the battles they moved on to fight somewhere else. Towns were built in the conquered territories with Roman lords in charge. Just in case the Britons felt like revolting, the Romans let retired Roman soldiers settle in the land outside the towns – a circle of trusted men to warn of danger. And, if the beaten Brits *did* give trouble then the army could get back quickly to help by marching along the new Roman roads.

Your teachers will tell you all about the legions and what they wore and how they lived. But they don't know everything.

Test your teacher . . .

Ask your teacher these questions. Can they get more than 5 out of 10? Can you?

If you were a Roman soldier . . .
1 What would you wear under your leather kilt?
a nothing

b underpants

c fig leaves

2 Where would
you drive on
the Roman roads?
a on the right
b down the centre
c on the left

3 How long would you have to stay in the army once you joined?

a 25 years

b 5 years

c the rest of your life

I'M A CENTURIAN CENTURIAN

4 Who could you marry?

a anyone

b no one

c a Roman

5 Who paid for your uniform, weapons, food and burial?

a the emperor

b they were free

c you paid for them yourself out of your wages

6 How tall did you have to be?

a over 1.8 metres

b between 1.6 and 1.8 metres

c under 1.6 metres

7 What would you use instead of toilet paper?

a a sponge on the end of a stick, dipped in cold water

b your tunic

c the daily newspaper

8 Your spear (pilum) had a 60 cm metal head that would snap off after it hit something. Why?

a so the enemy couldn't pick up the spear and throw it back

b so you could put the metal head in your pocket when you were marching

c because the Roman armourers couldn't make the heads stay on

9 Why was one Roman Centurion called "Give me another"?

a because he liked his soldiers to sing as they marched. When they'd finished one song he'd call out, "Give me another!"

b because he was greedy. After eating a pig's head he'd cry out, "Give me another!"

c because he cruelly beat his soldiers so hard he smashed his canes and had to call out, "Give me another!"

10 Why would the army doctor not notice your screams as he treated your wounds?

a because he enjoyed making you suffer

b because he was trained to carry on without paying attention to a soldier's cries

c because the Romans only employed deaf men as doctors

The rottenly clever Roman Army

The Romans were the best army in the ancient world because they used something their enemies didn't. The Romans used their brains! Are you as brainy?

Here are some problems the Romans overcame. What would you have done if you'd faced these problems . . .

1 Julius Caesar had a land army in Gaul (northern France). When the Veneti tribe there rebelled, they captured two Roman messengers and sailed off with them. Caesar quickly had ships built and followed. The Veneti were excellent sailors but poor fighters. Caesar needed a weapon that would stop the Veneti ships from sailing off while Roman soldiers climbed aboard. There was no gunpowder (for cannon or bullets). What simple (but very successful) weapon did the Romans make?

2 After the British Queen Boudicca was beaten, the Romans were able to move into the fenlands of East Anglia. The grass was rich but the land was very wet. If the Romans tried to wade through the swamps, the local tribes ambushed them. Then a new general arrived from Italy's Pontine marshes. He showed the soldiers how to get through swamps without wading up to their waists in water. What did he teach them?

3 In the early days of the Roman Republic, the Romans came up against the Greek king, Pyrrhus. The Greek strategy was to go into battle led by elephants. The elephants would charge at the Romans, trample them and send them running. But the Romans learned quickly. At the battle of Beneventum they found a way to face an elephant charge . . . and win! What would *you* do?

4 Some of the young men in the conquered lands did not want to fight in the Roman Army. It meant leaving their homes, farms and families to fight (and maybe die) in some distant corner of the world. The young men cut off the thumb of their right hand so they couldn't hold a sword. If they couldn't hold a sword then they wouldn't be expected to fight in the Roman Army. The Roman generals realised that all of these thumbless young men were trying to outwit them. What was their solution?

5 One day, Emperor Hadrian went to the public baths where his skin was carefully cleaned by slaves with scrapers. He saw an old man rubbing his back against a column. The old man was one of Hadrian's old soldiers. Hadrian asked why he was rubbing himself against the marble. The old man said it was because he couldn't afford a slave with a scraper. Hadrian gave the man slaves and money. BUT . . . next day the public baths were full of old men rubbing their backs against the marble! They were obviously scrounging for a Hadrian handout! What would you do if you were Hadrian?

Answers:

1 The Romans attached hooked knives onto the ends of long poles. As they neared the Veneti ships, the Romans slashed the enemy ropes and sails to stop them sailing. They then climbed aboard the Veneti boats and overpowered the sailors. The leaders were executed and the sailors sold for slavery.

2 How to use stilts! They were a great success at first. Eventually the tribes of the fens learned to knock the Romans off the stilts and stab them as they fell. Ah, well, it seemed like a brilliant idea at the time!

3 The Roman front line split in two. The elephants charged harmlessly through the line. They were too clumsy for the drivers to stop and turn. The helpless riders just kept going to the back of the Roman Army, where there were special troops waiting with long, sharp spears. They jabbed the elephants until the maddened creatures turned round and charged back again. The elephants flattened the Greek army, who weren't expecting them!

4 Cut off their heads! Anyone trying to avoid army service was sentenced to death. The young men soon learned this new law and decided to fight – possible death in war was better than certain death by execution. The Romans also branded or tattooed unwilling soldiers – if the soldier deserted, then he would have trouble hiding the fact that he was supposed to be in the army.

5 Hadrian simply told the old men to rub each other!

Make the punishment fit the crime

If you think punishments at school are hard, then how would you like to have been in the Roman Army? The barbarian armies charged at the Romans like bulls at a matador – and we know who usually wins *that* contest. The Roman Army had "discipline". They did what they were told, every time. And if they didn't do as they were told – no matter how small the offence – they had to be punished. Try to guess which crime earned which punishment . . .

CRIME	PUNISHMENT
I LAZINESS	A. DECIMATION OF A UNIT – I MAN IN EVERY X IS EXECUTED
II FALLING ASLEEP ON DUTY	B. SLEEP OUTSIDE THE SAFETY OF THE CAMP
III RUNNING AWAY IN A BATTLE	C. GET THE WORST FOOD – ROUGH BARLEY INSTEAD OF GOOD CORN
IV PUTTING YOUR UNIT IN DANGER	D. DEATH BY BEATING
V RUNNING AWAY WITH YOUR UNIT	E. DEATH BY STONING

Answer: 1B. 2C. 3D. 4E. 5A (Your unit would throw the stones). 5A ('The unlucky one in ten was chosen by drawing lots).

Let the reward fit the action

Of course there were *good* sides to being a Roman soldier too – otherwise no one would have wanted to join the army! The goodies were . . .

1 The army took two parts of every seven you earned in wages and saved it for you. When you retired they gave you all your savings and a piece of land. You could retire in comfort . . . if you lived long enough.

2 You could make extra wealth by robbing the countries you defeated. You could take money, animals or even living prisoners that you could sell for slaves.

I THINK I'VE GOT THE SACK

3 For brave actions there were no medals – there were crowns:

a a crown of oak leaves – for saving the life of a fellow citizen (Caesar won one at Mytilene when he was just 20 years old)

b a crown of plaited grass – for rescuing an army under siege

c a crown of gold – for being the first soldier over the wall of an enemy town

Don't get sick!

Roman doctors knew how to . . .

- AMPUTATE MANGLED LIMBS
- REMOVE TONSILS
- MEND BROKEN BONES

NEXT!

BUT – Roman doctors didn't know about anaesthetics (to put you to sleep while they hacked you about!).

Roman doctors could make medicines to cure sickness.

BUT – they had to mix them with honey to try to disguise the disgusting tastes.

Did you know?

A Roman legionary always went into battle with a first-aid kit of bandages and healing herbs?

THE CUT-THROAT CELTS

The Britons were part of the Celtic peoples. At one time the Celts had roamed round the world as much as the Romans did. One man put an end to all that – the Roman emperor, Julius Caesar.

The Celts used to fight fiercely for their tribal chiefs. But the tribes often fought *against* each other when they should have been fighting *together* against Julius Caesar. They needed one strong leader to bring them all together. But when that leader arrived it was too late.

Vercingetorix was a Celtic chief who was just as clever as Caesar at fighting and leading. Would you have been as clever as Vercingetorix? Here are some of the problems he faced. Could you have solved them?

Vercingetorix v Caesar

1 You meet the chiefs of the tribes every day to plan your war against Caesar. One of the chiefs argues against you. What do you do about him?

a Say to him, "Look, my friend, we must all stick together if we want to beat the rotten Romans. So, please, trust me. Remember, united we stand but divided we fall."

b Get upset. Say, "If you're going to argue with me you can find yourselves another leader. I'll fight Caesar by myself. When I've beaten him I'll beat you next. You'll be sorry!"

c Don't get upset. Simply have his ears cut off and one of his eyes gouged out. Send him back to his tribe with the message, "This is what you get if you mess with Vercingetorix!"

2 Caesar is a long way from home and a long way from fresh supplies. The Romans need food for the soldiers and their horses. They are getting it from the Celtic towns in the region of the Bituriges tribe. What can you do to stop them?

a Tell the Bituriges' chief to burn his towns to the ground and send his people to live with other tribes.
b Tell the Bituriges' chief to destroy all the food in the towns but let the people stay.
c Tell the Bituriges' chief to burn his towns to the ground but move all the people to the capital city of Avaricum.

3 Your tactics are working. Caesar is getting desperate for food. He sets off for Avaricum, which is the region's grain depot. How can you defend Avaricum against Caesar's army?
a Build a wooden wall.
b Build a stone wall with a ditch in front.
c Build a brick wall.

4 Caesar begins to build towers on wheels to push up to the walls. When these towers reach the walls the Romans will let down a drawbridge at the top and swarm over your walls. What can you do?
a Build an even taller tower behind your walls and throw down fireballs on top of them.
b Leave the town and attack Caesar's towers.
c Run away.

5 Caesar cannot get the towers near the walls because there is a ditch in front of the walls. He sends soldiers into the forest to chop down trees. He rolls the logs into the ditch and begins to fill it up.

What can you do to stop the Romans filling the ditch?

a Dig a tunnel under your walls and set fire to the logs?

b Surrender.

c Send a raiding party out to steal the Roman axes so they can't chop down any more trees.

6 The Romans manage to get towers up to the walls. You would like to set fire to them but the clever Romans have covered them with leather, which doesn't catch fire very easily. What can you throw at them instead?

a dead horses

b boiling fat and tar

c cold water.

7 Despite your efforts the Romans reach the walls. They catch hold of the top of the wall with hooks, and swarm up the ropes attached to the hooks. What's the best defence against this?

a Throw the hooks back.

b Pull the hooks up and drag them inside your fort.

c Wait for the Romans to climb them and try to kill them as they reach the top.

8 During the Roman assault it begins to rain heavily. What do your defenders do?
a Run for shelter until the rain stops and hope the Romans do the same.
b Fight on and get wet.
c Ask the Romans for a cease-fire until the weather improves.

9 The Romans reach the streets of Avaricum. They begin slaughtering every man, woman and child in sight. What should Vercingetorix do?
a Give himself up.
b Fight to the death.
c Make sure his best fighting men escape through a back entrance.

10 Vercingetorix reaches the safety of Alesia. The Romans are following. You have a large army. What should you do with it?
a Send most of the army away to gather help from other Celtic tribes and keep just a few to defend Alesia.
b Keep all the soldiers in Alesia and hope that help will arrive.
c Leave the army in Alesia and go for help yourself?

Vercingetorix's ten steps to Rome, or, Answers:

1 Vercingetorix could not afford to show any weakness or he'd be killed by the other Celtic chiefs. He could not plead (**1a**) or sulk (**1b**). He had to show he meant business and would make an example of anyone who opposed him (**1c**).

2 Vercingetorix made just one mistake. He couldn't destroy the supplies and leave the people in the towns (**2b**) – the warriors would not have fought if they knew the Romans had captured their wives and children. He should have destroyed the supplies AND the towns (**2a**). If you chose **2a** then you'd have been a crueller but better leader than Vercingetorix! But the Bituriges were proud of Avaricum. They pleaded with Vercingetorix not to destroy it. He weakened and agreed (**2c**). From then on he was pretty well doomed.

3 Vercingetorix had fought the Romans for years and knew their way of fighting. They would have simply burned a wooden wall (**3a**) and battered down a brick wall (**3c**). The best wall was a solid stone wall with a ditch in front (**3b**).

4 Caesar wasn't put out by the solid walls of Avaricum. He began building towers. Vercingetorix expected this and didn't give up (**4c**). Of course, he didn't leave the safety of the town and attack the Romans in open battle (**4b**) because that's exactly what they wanted. He just ordered bigger towers to be built behind his own walls (**4a**).

5 Caesar could defeat the ditch by filling it with

new logs. Vercingetorix couldn't stop him (**5c**) but didn't let it beat him (**5b**). The Bituriges were good iron miners and so could dig shafts. They dug one under the Roman logs and set fire to them (**5a**). This delayed the Roman attack . . . but failed to stop it.

6 The Celtic soldiers knew that the only thing that would slow down the Roman towers wasn't anything solid (**6a**), but liquid, which would run through the joins in the Roman "umbrella". Cold water wasn't going to hurt them (**6c**) but boiling tar and oil would. This is what they did (**6b**).

7 The Romans were determined – and getting hungrier! They began to use grappling hooks to climb the walls. There was no point in throwing them back (**7a**) because the Romans would just try again at another spot. No one had been able to stop the Romans by trying to kill them at the top (**7c**) because there were just too many of them. Clever Vercingetorix devised the plan of hauling up the hooks and taking away the Roman weapons (**7b**)!

8 When a rain-storm hit Avaricum, all of Vercingetorix's cleverness was undone by the stupidity of his men. They should have fought on (**8b**). The Romans wouldn't let some rain stop them (**8c**) and it was no use expecting them to. The defenders ran for shelter (**8a**). The Romans leapt over the walls.

9 Vercingetorix knew that the battle for Avaricum was lost, but the war wasn't. He wasn't going to give up (**9a**). On the other hand there was no point in waiting to be killed (**9b**) when there were new Celtic armies waiting to fight. All he had to do was to escape with the soldiers and fight again (**9c**). Unfortunately, the women who were being left behind to be massacred didn't like the idea. Not surprising really! They began wailing and screaming. This gave the escape plan away to the Romans and they hurried to cut off the escape route. The Romans massacred 40,000 Avaricum people. Only Vercingetorix and 800 others escaped to fight another day.

10 Vercingetorix reached the safety of Alesia with a new large army. If he'd tried to keep the army with him (**10b**) they'd have eaten the supplies in no time and starved to death before help arrived. He couldn't get to all the dozens of tribes himself to get help (**10c**) so he sent his troops to different Celtic tribes and kept just enough to defend the town (**10a**).

It almost worked. A huge Celtic army arrived. But the Romans had built a ring of defences round the town. The soldiers in Alesia couldn't get out. The new Celtic army couldn't get in. They gave up and went away.

Vercingetorix was trapped. He gave himself up to his own people and said they could do what they needed. The Romans wanted Vercingetorix alive – that was how the Celts delivered him. In 45 BC he was paraded through the streets of Rome . . . then executed. The Celts on the continent were crushed. They survived mainly in the islands off the shores of Europe. The British Islands. If Caesar wanted to finish them off, then he had to invade Britain . . . which he did.

That's why it's thought that the defeat of Vercingetorix led to the Roman invasion of Britain! If Vercingetorix had only destroyed Avaricum (as in **2a**) then we might never have had a Roman Britain!

Heads you win, heads you lose

Heads were popular with the Celtic race to which the Britons belonged. Here are ten horrible brainless facts . . .

1 In 500 BC, the British tribespeople believed that the head had magical powers. They thought that severed heads could utter prophecies and warnings, especially if they were in groups of three.

2 Rotting human heads were stuck on poles at the entrance to a hill fort.

3 Heads could be thrown into a lake or river as a gift to the gods.

4 After a battle the Celts rode from the battlefield with the heads of enemies dangling from the necks of their horses.

5 The heads might then be nailed to the walls of their houses.

6 Sometimes they were preserved in cedar oil and taken out years later to show off to visitors. A Roman visitor said that the Britons would not part with their lucky heads for their weight in gold.

7 The Celtic Boii Tribe of the Po Valley (Northern Italy) took skulls and covered them in gold. They would then be used as cups!

8 Heads featured in many ornaments of stone, metal or wood and paintings. Severed heads could be seen staring at you from the surface of tiles, pots, sword hilts, chariot fittings and even bucket handles!

9 Because the gods were more powerful than humans, they often had more heads. An Irish goddess, Ellen, had three heads! The druids had to keep her constantly supplied with sacrifices to stop her coming out of her underworld cave and ravaging the land.

10 The Britons even told stories about the magical power of the head. Many legends involved severed heads.

A typical story is the Welsh legend of Bran the Blessed . . .

DAILY HEADLINE NEWS

HEADITOR : M.T. SKULL

BIG BRAN'S NOGGIN NICKED!

Some treacherous troublemaker has taken Britain's greatest treasure!

Yesterday the London burial place of Bran the Blessed was robbed. The great warrior's head was later found to be missing, along with another two skulls from the graveyard. The authorities are looking for a man with three heads!

Magical

As all our readers will know, the head of Bran the Blessed was the most magical article in the whole of Britain. Eighty years ago Bran was mortally wounded in a bloody battle with an Irish king. As he lay dying he ordered the seven surviving soldiers to cut off his head and carry it with them. This they did and they found themselves in the after-life as the guest of Bran – even though they weren't dead!

Then one warrior disobeyed one of Big Bran's orders. He opened a forbidden door. The warriors were heaved out of heaven. But, before they went, one of them tucked Bran's head up his tunic. And so it returned to earth. The head was buried in London, where it would guard Britain against evil for ever more.

Reward

Now it has been stolen there's no knowing what might happen. *The Daily Headline News* is offering a reward for information leading to its return. Otherwise Britain will be heading for disaster!

Did you know?

The Romans sometimes treated slaves brutally in their conquered territories and in Rome itself. In AD 157 the Roman writer Apuleius described life in a rotten Roman flour mill . . .

> *The slaves were poor, skinny things. Their skin was black and blue with bruises, their backs were covered with cuts from the whip. They wore rags, not clothes, and hardly enough to keep them decent. They had a brand mark burned into their forehead and half of their hair was shaved off. They wore chains around their ankles.*

A slave revolt was led by Spartacus at a gladiator school near Naples. The slaves formed a huge army and terrorised the area for a couple of years. At last a Roman army defeated them. Over 6000 slaves were crucified along the side of the main road from Capua to Rome.

YOU JUST CAN'T GET THE STAFF THESE DAYS

THE BATTLING BRITONS

If you weren't a Roman then the Romans called you "barbarian" – or stranger. This was because the Romans didn't understand the language of strange peoples. They said they sounded like sheep – "bah-bah-bah" people ... bah-bah-rians ... barbarians, get it?

So, when the Romans arrived in Britain they met "barbarians". But the Britons weren't "barbarous" – they weren't rough, crude, simple people. They were simply "different". Still, they *did* have one or two habits that you won't find in your school today ...

WOW! THESE PEOPLE ARE DIFFERENT!

ER.. THAT'S ACTUALLY A SHEEP MARCUS

The British way of life . . . and death

1 The Britons had priests called Druids. Druids led the worship of the gods of Nature. An important time of year was Beltane – 21 March – when night and day are exactly 12 hours each. If people wanted the days to keep getting longer, and summer to come, then they had to give the gods something they would like. The Druids thought that the gods would like nothing better than a severed head ... so the Druids had a victim's head chopped off.

2 The Britons lived in forts with huge earth walls. They built one called Maiden Castle in the south of England. The Britons would feast there on joints of pork. They got rid of the bones by throwing them over their shoulders. When the piles of bones became too deep, they levelled them out and spread a fresh layer of earth and chalk over the top.

3 The men wore long moustaches which trapped food as they ate. A fussy Roman writer called Diodorus wrote, "Their drink passes through their moustaches like a strainer!" Yuk!

4 At a British tribal feast the guests would sit on animal skins on the floor, eat with their fingers . . . and keep on eating! When they were tired, they just rolled over onto the skin carpet and fell asleep.

5 The Britons weren't as filthy as they sound from this. They used to wash with soap long before the Romans did.

AND ANOTHER THING, THOSE ROMANS DON'T HALF PONG!

6 In battle, Celtic warriors often fought without any clothes at all. The Romans said that the Britons were painted from head to toe in a blue dye called woad . . . but maybe they were just blue with the cold!

7 The Celts believed in staying thin and fit. If a young warrior became too tubby for a normal sized belt then he was fined.

8 The Britons were related to the Celtic tribes of Gaul (northern France) who were feared by the Romans for their fierceness. And not only the men! Marcellinus said . . .

> *A whole troop of foreigners would not be able to withstand a Gaul if he called for his wife to help him. Swelling her neck, gnashing her teeth and swinging her white arms of enormous size she begins to strike blows mixed with kicks as if they were missiles sent from the string of a catapult.*

9 The Celtic men were proud of their hair. They bleached it by washing it in lime. The roots of the hair would be dark and the rest a bleached blond. The lime also made the hair stand on end. They went into battle with their hair in a crest of spikes. One writer said the spikes were so stiff and strong that you could have stuck an apple on the end of each point! And they didn't wear helmets that could save their life in a battle – it would have spoiled their hairstyle!

HAS ANYONE SEEN MY LIME HAIR GEL?

10 Brave British women must have looked as fearsome as their blue warrior men. They painted their fingernails, reddened their cheeks with a herb called ruan and darkened their eyebrows with the juice of berries.

But the boldest of British women – maybe the bravest ever – was Queen Boudicca.

That was what the Britons called her. Later generations changed her name to Boadicea. Some people say this change was made because Boadicea sounded nicer. Another story is that a mediaeval monk made a spelling mistake when he was copying an old history and his mistake was copied by later historians! Let's call her Boudicca . . .

Boudicca, *This is Your Life!*

1 Boudicca always looked pretty fearsome with her huge mop of bright red hair, her rough voice and her king-sized body. A Roman writer, Cassius Dio, said . . .

She was very tall. Her eyes seemed to stab you. Her voice was harsh and loud. Her thick, reddish-brown hair hung down below her waist. She always wore a great golden torc [band] around her neck and a flowing tartan cloak fastened with a brooch.

BOUDICCA

2 She married Prasutagus, King of the Iceni tribe of Britons. They had two daughters. Prasutagus, the wimp, didn't fancy fighting the Romans when they arrived. Instead he tried to make a deal with the emperor: "When I die the Iceni lands can be split between you and my daughters." Then he did a stupid and wimpy thing – he died.

3 The Roman Army simply took over. The officers ran the country while the slaves plundered the Iceni houses. Then the Romans made a BIG mistake. They had Big Boudicca whipped. Big Boud was not amused.

4 The Romans had whipped Boudicca . . . so Boudicca whipped up a rebellion. The revolting Britons captured the Roman town of Camulodunum (now called Colchester in Essex).

5 The gods appeared to be on Big Boud's side. They gave the Brits several "signs" that they were on the side of the Iceni.

- The Roman statue of Victory fell down . . . face down as if it were fleeing from the attackers.
- Women reported that ghostly, ghastly shrieks could be heard in the Roman senate house and theatre.
- At the mouth of the Thames, a phantom town was seen in ruins.
- The sea turned blood red.
- As the tide went out, the sands took on the shape of corpses.

6 Big Boud marched on to Londinium (London) and Verulamium (St Albans) where her army did a lot of murdering and pillaging. In all they killed about 70,000 people.

7 One Roman didn't run away. Paulinus had just 10,000 soldiers to fight 100,000 Brits.

8 Big Boud rode round the Brit tribes in her war chariot and gave them her famous speech . . .

> *We British are used to women commanders in war. I am the daughter of mighty men. But I am not fighting for my royal power now . . . I am fighting as an ordinary person who has lost her freedom. I am fighting for my bruised body. The gods will grant us the revenge we deserve. Think of how many of us are fighting, and why. Then you will win this battle or die. That is what I, a woman, plan to do. Let the men live as slaves if they want. I won't!*

9 The 10,000 Romans were well organised. The 100,000 Britons charged around the way they always did. The result was a great victory for the Romans.

10 Big Boud faced another flogging. The Roman historian, Tacitus, said she took poison and died. The Roman historian, Dio, said she died of a disease. Believe whichever one you like . . . or neither. Perhaps she just died of a broken heart. Boudicca, that was your life!

Did you know?

The Roman historian, Tacitus, said the Britons had 80,000 warriors killed in Boudicca's final battle. That means each of the 10,000 Roman soldiers killed (on average) *eight* Britons! He claimed that only 400 Romans died so it took 250 Britons to kill just *one* Roman! No wonder the British lost!

Of course, the fact is that Tacitus was telling *fibs*. He wanted to tell the Roman world what a great army the Romans had and how brave their leaders were . . . after all, his father-in-law was one of those fighting in that battle!

So, DON'T believe everything you read in your history books. If the Brits had been able to write then, they would have given a very different account of the battle. The Romans were very good at blaming other people for things. The truth is usually that there are good arguments on both sides . . .

Who's to blame for Boudicca's battles?

Diary of disaster

One of the great heroes of the British tribes was Caratacus of the Catuvellauni tribe (north-west of London). While many tribal leaders were making peace with the Romans, Caratacus went on fighting. In the end he was defeated, of course. But he was still a hero.

That was one big difference. The Romans loved winners. The Britons seemed to love losers. The other difference was that the Romans learned from their mistakes. The Britons didn't.

It isn't likely that Caratacus could write. But, if he could, and if he kept a diary, would it have looked like this . . .?

Summer of 43 AD Kent

Disaster! I can't believe it! After two days of battle the Romans have defeated us. All we had to do was to stop them crossing the ~~Thames~~ River Medway. There's only one bridge over the Medway. All we had to do was sit tight on the northern end, wait for the Romans to cross it, then cut them into pieces...

... We'd have killed them in their thousands. We would! But what did they do ??? They cheated !!! They sent troops upstream, they crossed where the water was shallow and attacked us from the back. That's not fair, is it?

Of course, we could have run them down with our chariots. We could! But what did they do? They cheated again!

They shot our horses. That's not fair, is it? They even killed my brother, Togodumnus. Poor, stupid Toggy. He should have done what I did. Retreated. Like dad always said, "He who fights and runs away, lives to fight another day."

So, I'm alive and next time I'll stuff those rotten Romans !!!!

Late Summer of 43 AD - Dorset

Disaster! Again! The Romans are marching west. They're taking our hill-forts one after another. Of course, they don't fight fair. ~~Te~~ They don't fight man to man ~~s~~ and let us kill them....

No. They shoot at our defenders with iron-tipped arrows. Hundreds at a time from some big machine. They drive us off the walls then swarm in after we've taken shelter.

They've taken 20 hill-forts that way. I never thought I'd live to see the day they'd take the mighty Maiden Castle. In fact I nearly didn't live to see today! I just managed to retreat in time. He who fights and runs away.... But I'll stay in England. They'll never drive me into Wales.. Never!!

The other leaders are all surrendering. making peace and getting fat. But they won't get a hero like me. Not like they got poor old Toggy... ~~tet~~ Next time !!! get them...

Summer of 48 AD - Wales

Who is the greatest British leader??
Caratacus. Me! Alright, so I'm stuck in the
wild, wet Welsh mountains. But every now and
then I lead a raid on some Roman troops
and crack a few rotten Roman heads.

Actually it's rather hard to crack a Roman
head. They wear these metal helmets. <u>That's not</u>
fair, that's not. Some people might even call
it <u>cheating</u>!

They'd like to drive me up to North Wales
and into the Irish Sea. Well, there is absolutely
<u>NO</u> chance of that. My men will fight to ~~the~~
the death (Not <u>my</u> death of course. They
need me alive to lead them)

I'll end up in North Wales over my warriors'
dead bodies !!!

North
Wales

Nth England

Welsh
mountains

Dorset

Kent

51

North Wales - 51 AD

Disaster! Again!!! I never thought I'd see the day when the Romans would take a fort like Llanymynech. But they did. I still can't believe it. They couldn't attack Llanymynech from the back because that's a steep mountain face. They couldn't attack it from the front because that's the river Vrynwy and the front wall of the fort.

But they did it! They crossed the river then came to the wall. We were pouring spears and stones and ~~and~~ arrows down on their heads. We should have massacred them...

So, what did they do? They cheated, us usual. They put their shields over their heads and came close together. The shields formed a solid wall over them. (They copied this from a Roman animal with a shell called a "tortoise" or something)

Our weapons just bounced off their "shell" and the Romans just kept coming till everyone was captured. The rotten Romans even took my family! I was lucky to escape. He who fights and runs away...... Still, next time I'll get them. I'm going to join forces with Queen Cartimandua of the Brigantes up near York ....

..... They're the biggest tribe outside of Roman rule. With **me** to lead them we'll chase the Romans all the way back to Rome. And they can take their tortoises with them.

I even hear old Claudius brought some huge grey monsters called <u>elephants</u> with him. They can take <u>them</u> back too!!! This time next year I'll be in Rome!!!

North England – later in 51 AD

Life with Queen Cartimandua is great! I don't even miss my poor captured family. The beautiful Carti obviously fancies me. Can't blame her really. Me being the gretest British hero ever seen.

Loads of food^ Better than living like an outlaw in the hills. And bads of wine. Lovely stuff. The very besht Roman wine. I wonder where she gets it from?

And she's even decorating me with chains. Chains on my wrists. Chains on my ankles. I fink that Carti loves me show mush she wantsh to keep me here forever!!! I'm very shleepy now.

Nighty night Carti dear!

53

Next day

My head hurts. And worse. Much worse
I'm a prisoner. I've found out where that
treacherous, ugly, vicious, lying Queen gets
her Roman wine from. She gets it from
the Romans !!! And what does she give
the Romans in return?

Me! I've been handed over to the Romans.
They're ~~taking~~ taking me back to Rome. It's curtains
for Caratacus! I said I'd be in Rome within
a year, I never thought it would be in
chains. It's a disaster! They'll execute
me for sure. Me the greatest living British
hero. I'm not afraid to die of course ... I just
don't want to be there when it happens.
· · · · · ·

Next week - middle of the English Channel

I think I'm going to be sea-s...

Next month - Rome

What a place! These Romans really know how to treat a hero! Met old Claudius the emperor. Messy little weedy fellow. Dribbles and slobbers and limps about the place. But a very powerful man. Most important man in the world I reckon. And he spoke to me! (I didn't understand a word, of course, because he was blabbering away in Latin. But I could tell he was pleased to see me!)

Claudi gave an order and my chains were cut off. I thought, Aha! This is it! ~~You're~~ You're for the chop, Caratacus. But no! They treated me like a hero. They even said I was free to live in Rome. I think I might just do that. There are huge buildings all made of stone and marble. I've never seen anything like it.

Who wants to live in cold wet Britain in a draughty wooden hut? Not me! After all, I am the greatest British hero ever. I reckon I've earned an easy life with my old mate Claudi. Maybe the rotten Romans aren't so rotten after all !!!

The diary might be imaginary but the facts are about right. Caratacus arrived in Rome and told the Romans that they could only have great victories if they had great warriors (like himself) to fight against. "If you execute me, then all your glory will be forgotten," he warned them. Claudius agreed and released him.

But Caratacus was still puzzled when he saw the wealth of Rome. "When you Romans have all this, why do you want our poor huts?" Good question.

Meanwhile, back in Britain, the treacherous Cartimandua stayed in power (with Roman help) for another 15 years. Then her husband attacked her and kicked her out. The Romans really did take the British forts with ease. The Romans made mistakes. But they didn't usually make the same mistake twice. That's what made them so successful.

Test your teacher

"Please sir/miss/gorilla-features! Where is Boudicca's body now? Is it . . .
a Under her statue on Westminster Bridge (opposite the Houses of Parliament),
b Under platform 8 of King's Cross Station,
c Somewhere at the bottom of the Thames?"

56

Did you know?

A mysterious funeral ceremony took place near London in the second century AD. A grave has been discovered in an underground room but it contains no human bodies. There are just two carvings of men who look like Roman senators. Historians think that these men must have died during fighting and were buried elsewhere. It seems that they did not have an honourable burial . . . maybe they were traitors. Whatever the reason their carved heads were walled up in this room to be forgotten. But one body was found in the tomb – the body of the family cat!

57

ROTTEN ROMAN LEADERS

Julius Caesar was one of the greatest Roman leaders. He was so successful he was murdered . . . by his friend! Rome had been run as a "republic" for many years. That is to say the important people in Rome decided what to do. Then Julius Caesar became so powerful there was a fear that he'd take over. The people thought he wanted to become "King of the Romans".

The last king they'd had was a disaster. His name was Tarquinius Superbus who lived in the 5th century BC. He abolished certain rights of Romans and was the rottenest Roman of the time.

Was it true that Caesar wanted to be crowned king? And would he get to be as bad as Tarquinius? If so, it would be better to kill him now! This is how it happened . . .

Caesar's sticky end

1 Caesar had himself elected "Dictator for life" . . . that was just another way of saying the dreaded word "King"!
2 Caesar started wearing red boots! Only a king wore red boots.

3 At a festival, Mark Antony, Caesar's friend, offered Caesar a diadem – a small crown. Caesar took it off – a sign that he didn't want to be king, perhaps? The crowds cheered when he took it off. But did Caesar and Mark Antony set this up to find out how the people felt? What if the people had cheered when the crown had been put *on?*

4 Caesar was due to speak to the Senate (the Roman parliament) on 15 March, 44 BC. Straight after his speech he was due to lead his troops into battle. During a war he'd be surrounded by his soldiers. No one could kill him then. If he was to die then he had to die on 15 March.

5 Caesar was a great believer in "fate" – if he was going to die then there was nothing he could do to change his fortune. A fortune-teller told Caesar not to go to the Senate on 15 March. It didn't stop him.

6 Caesar's wife asked him not to go to the Senate that day. She'd had terrible nightmares and a feeling that something bad would happen. That didn't stop him.

7 Caesar felt ill on the morning of 15 March and was almost too ill to attend the Senate . . . he was worse by the time he left!

8 The killers chose Brutus as their leader. Brutus was one of the most popular men in Rome. He was famous for being honest. If he led the killing then the people of Rome would know the murderers were "honest" – that they did it for the good of the people.

9 On the evening of 14 March someone asked Caesar, "What sort of death would you like?" Caesar answered, "A sudden one." He got his wish.

When Caesar entered the Senate the senators all stood up as a sign of respect. Some of Brutus' gang slipped behind Caesar's chair while others came to meet him. Cimber grabbed Caesar's robe with both hands and pulled it from his neck. This was the signal for the attack.

Casca struck the first blow. His knife made a wound in Caesar's neck, but not a serious one, so that Caesar could still turn around, grab the knife, and hold on.

The watchers were horrified. They didn't dare run away or help Caesar or even make a sound.

Each assassin bared his dagger now. They all closed in on Caesar in a circle. They pushed him this way and that, like a wild beast surrounded by hunters.

Brutus stabbed Caesar in the groin. Above all Caesar had trusted Brutus.

Some say Caesar defended himself against all the rest – but when he saw Brutus coming at him with a dagger, he pulled his robe over his head and sank down.

The attackers pushed Caesar against the statue of his old enemy, Pompey. The statue became drenched with blood.

Caesar received 23 wounds.

Many of the assassins wounded each other as they fought to stick so many knives into one body.

The killers made one big mistake. They didn't kill Mark Antony at the same time. "Honest" Brutus said it would be wrong. They were only out to stop wicked Caesar from becoming king. But it was Mark Antony who led a campaign of vengeance that destroyed the killers. Brutus committed suicide when he was defeated by Mark Antony at Philippi in 42 BC.

Caesar had left most of his fortune to his grand-nephew, Octavian. Young Octavian became the sort of dictator that Caesar wanted to be. The thing the Romans feared – rule by one all-powerful man – had returned. And some of the emperors that followed were a hundred times worse than Julius Caesar!

In fact, some of the Roman Emperors were pretty weird. Here are the Rottenest Romans of all . . .

Emperor Tiberius

Ruled: 14 AD–37 AD

Favourite saying: "I don't care if they hate me . . . so long as they obey me!" (Know any teachers like that?)

Nastiest habit: Breaking the legs of anyone who disobeyed him.

Rottenest act: Tiberius needed a holiday. "I think I'll take a break!" he announced. As the servants scuttled off to find their shinpads he cried, "A holiday, I mean. A short break on the island of Capri off the south coast of Italy would be very nice."

He had only been there a few days when a humble Capri fisherman caught a large crab and a huge mullet fish. The poor man decided that it would make a wonderful gift for the visiting emperor.

The cliff was steep and there was no track. The mullet was heavy. The fisherman struggled for an hour and finally reached the top.

"Take me to the emperor," he pleaded with the guard.

"The emperor wishes to be left alone today," the guard said, shaking his head.

"It's the biggest mullet I've ever caught!" the fisherman said proudly. "The gods meant it for the emperor. Tell the emperor I must see him!"

The guard shrugged. It was a boring life, standing

on the top of the cliff watching the gulls. The emperor might order him to break the fisherman's legs. "I'll see what the emperor says," he smirked.

Five minutes later he returned and said with a grin. "The emperor will see you now."

The poor little man dragged the huge fish into the emperor's room. "You'll be sorry," the guard muttered.

As the fisherman stepped through the door two huge guards grabbed his arms. "I've brought a gift for the emperor!" he squeaked.

Tiberius stepped forward. "You disturbed my rest, you smelly little man!" he snarled.

"It's the fish, your worship!" the fisherman cried.

"No!" the emperor jeered. "That fish smells sweeter than you. Guards!"

"Sir?"

"Sweeten the little man. Rub that fish over his body!"

"It was a present . . . ouch! Mullet scales are very rough!" he screamed.

The guard scrubbed the rough skin over the fisherman's face till the skin was scraped off and his face left raw and bleeding. The guard smiled as he stripped the skin off the fisherman's chest.

"Ahh! Oooh!" the man wailed.

"Enough!" the emperor snapped. The guards let the fisherman fall to the floor where he lay groaning and muttering something through his bleeding lips.

"What did you say?" Tiberius growled.

"I just said thank the gods I didn't bring you that big crab I caught this morning," the little man burbled.

The emperor's eyes lit up with evil glee. "Go to this man's house and fetch the crab," he chuckled.

The guard nodded. As he left the emperor's room he winked at the sobbing fisherman. "I told you that you'd be sorry."

And after being scrubbed with the sharp shell of a crab the little man was so sorry that he wished he'd never been born.

Sticky end: Tiberius died at the age of 78, probably suffocated by his chief helper. The Roman people went wild with joy!

Caligula

Ruled: 37 AD–41 AD

Favourite sayings: To his friends at a banquet, "It has just occurred to me that I only have to give one nod and your throats will be cut."

To the guards of a row of criminals, "Kill every man between that one with the bald head and that one over there."

To his people, "Rome is a city of necks just waiting for me to chop."

To everyone who would listen, "I am a god."

Nastiest habit: His little "jokes". At a sacrifice ceremony he was given a hammer which would knock out the beast to be sacrificed. The priest was waiting to cut the beast's throat. Caligula hit the priest over the head instead!

Rottenest act: Caligula loved to organize huge killing festivals with loads of spectators. There were fights to the death between gladiators, and fights with wild animals. But the wild animals had to be kept alive until the day of the contest. Caligula was shocked at the cost of the raw meat needed to feed the animals. So he found a cheap supply of meat . . . he fed criminals to them!

Daftest act: He made his dear friend Incitatus a consul – so Incitatus became one of the most powerful rulers in the Roman Empire. So? So, Incitatus was his favourite *horse!*

Sticky end: One of his trusted guards stabbed him to death. Others went to the palace where they killed his wife and child.

Claudius

Ruled: 41 AD–54 AD

Favourite saying: "K-k-k-k-k-k-. . . er . . . execute him!"

Nastiest habit: Watching criminals being tortured and men being executed by being flogged to death.

Rottenest act: Claudius discovered his wife was a bit of a flirt and had wild parties with her friends. Claudius not only had *her* executed but 300 party friends went too.

Sticky end: His niece, Agrippina, poisoned him with mushrooms.

Nero

Ruled: 54 AD–68 AD

Favourite sayings: He played the lyre very badly but people told him he was brilliant. The Greeks were particularly creepy about telling him he was good. "Only the Greeks are worth my genius," he would say.

When he knew he had to die all he could say was, "What a loss I shall be to the art of music!"

Nastiest habit: Murdering people. He had his half-brother, Britannicus, poisoned. (Actually, Britannicus had a food taster who ate and drank a tiny bit of every dish that the Emperor was going to eat. If the food was poisoned, the taster would die first. The taster drank some hot wine and passed it over to the emperor. The taster was fine. The wine was "safe" to drink. But Britannicus complained that the wine was too hot and ordered water to cool it. *Then* he drank it . . . and died. The cold *water* had been poisoned!)

Nero had his first wife, Octavia, murdered. Her head was sent to Nero's new girlfriend, Poppaea. But then he murdered Poppaea, too.

Nero had Christians persecuted cruelly . . .

- They would be tied to a post, covered in tar and set alight.
- They would be covered in animal skins and thrown to hungry, wild dogs.
- They were crucified in large numbers.

Rottenest act: Agrippina had poisoned Claudius and now her son, Nero, was emperor. She thought she could rule the empire through her weak and wicked son.

Nero had other ideas. His mother was always interfering – stopping his meeting with his girlfriend, Acte, because she wasn't royal. Agrippina had to go.

First he made up their row over Acte. Then he invited mum to join him at a party on the Bay of Naples. Agrippina was happy to accept, glad to be friends with her son once more.

Nero sent a boat to pick her up. A special boat with special oarsmen. For the boat was designed to fall apart at sea and the oarsmen were instructed not to let Agrippina return alive. The boat set off on a beautiful starry night.

But the boat didn't fall apart. There were heavy weights on the wooden canopy over Agrippina's seat. At the right moment they were to crash through the canopy, kill Agrippina and fall through the bottom of the boat to sink it. Everyone would say the boat hit a rock. Sad accident. Poor Nero, losing his loving mother.

That's what was *meant* to happen. But, when the weights fell through the roof they killed Agrippina's friend. Agrippina and her other friend, Aceronnia, escaped . . . and the boat didn't sink!

The oarsmen tried to rock the boat to capsize it. That's when Aceronnia did a very brave thing. She began to cry out, "Save me! I am Agrippina, the emperor's mother! I am Agrippina!"

And in the darkness the oarsmen believed her. They battered her to death with their oars while the real Agrippina slipped over the side and escaped back to her palace. She sent a message to Nero saying what a lucky escape she'd had.

Nero was furious. He decided to make sure the next time. He sent two murderers to her palace. Agrippina thought they'd come from Nero to find out if she was all right!

As the first one battered her with a club she realised her mistake. When the other drew his sword she bared her stomach and invited him to stab her where the ungrateful Nero had come from. He did.

Nero reported that she had killed herself!

Sticky end: When he knew that the Roman Army had deserted him and rebels were coming to arrest him, he placed a sword to his throat. One of his friends gave him a push. The arresting officer **arrived as he bled to death.**

Ten funny facts about Roman emperors

1 Emperor Caligula's real name was Gaius. Caligula was just a nickname meaning "little boot". This was because he liked dressing up and playing at being a soldier from a very early age.

2 Caligula wanted to copy Julius Caesar and invade Britain. In 40 AD he went to the Roman base in Boulogne (in northern France) where he set sail to lead the invasion. He turned back when he saw that no one wanted to follow him!

3 Augustus Caesar was one of the more human emperors. But even he had his moments – the murder of Julius Caesar really upset him. As Suetonius said, "Augustus showed no mercy to his beaten enemies. He sent Brutus' head to Rome to be thrown at the feet of Caesar's statue."

4 Julius Caesar gave us our modern calendar. The early Romans had 12 months plus a 13th month that was added every four years. In 46 BC Caesar gave us the 12-month, 365-day year with the 29-day February leap year.

5 Emperor Heliogabalus enjoyed the hobby of collecting cobwebs . . . by the ton!

OF ALL MY BELGIAN COBWEBS THIS IS MY FAVOURITE

6 Honorius loved chickens. His favourite chicken was called Rome. He was hiding in his country mansion, safe from the invading army of Goths. When the city of Rome was overrun by Alaric and his army of Goths, a messenger arrived to say, "Rome is lost!" Honorius was heart-broken...

until someone told him the messenger meant the capital *city* and not the *hen*.

7 Nero enjoyed the cruel "circuses" so much that he had to take part. He was dressed in the skins of wild animals and locked in a cage. The human victims were tied to stakes in the arena. Nero's cage was opened. He leapt out and attacked the victims.

8 When Emperor Pertinax was murdered there wasn't just *one* person to take his place. *Two* men claimed the throne. Both men thought it would be useful to have the support of the emperor's praetorian guard – so they tried to outbid each other for it. Julianus won. He made an offer of 25,000 sesterces (Roman money) to each man. Unfortunately he couldn't afford to pay *all* the men in *all* the Roman armies across the world. They attacked and threw him out after just 66 days on the throne. The money he spent on bribing the emperor's guards was wasted – they were easily tricked into giving up their weapons.

9 In the 50 years between 235 AD and 285 AD there were about 20 emperors. Most of them were there a short time, murdered and replaced by the murderer who was murdered and replaced by the murderer, and so on. Some of the senior Romans refused to become emperor at this time – not surprising really!

10 Septimius had particularly nasty family problems. He had two sons, Caracalla and Geta. Caracalla was allowed to become joint emperor when he was just 13. Caracalla had his father-in-law murdered, then set off with his father and brother to conquer Scotland. During the campaign, Caracalla threatened to kill his father – but didn't. Old Septimius died in York and his dying words to his sons were, "Do not disagree with each other." Fat chance. Within a year Caracalla had brother Geta murdered. Caracalla was sole emperor at last. He kept the throne for five years, then . . . no prizes for guessing what happened to him. Yes, he was murdered.

Did you know?

Julius Caesar passed burial laws for the inhabitants of new towns built in the Roman Empire:

- "No one may bring, burn or bury a dead person within the boundaries of the town."
- "No crematorium shall be established within half a mile of a town."

(Burial sites had to be either outside the city walls or just within its limits. Caesar wanted a perfect town full of grand buildings and fresh air for his faithful followers.)

ROTTEN ROMAN CHILDHOOD

Children had a tough time in the age of the rotten Romans from the moment they were born. One writer, Soranus, described how each new-born child was laid on the earth and allowed to cry for a while before it was washed and clothed. Only the fit survived.

Some of the Germans in the Roman Empire gave their new-born children an even worse test. They dunked the child in cold water. If the baby came out purple with the cold or shivering then it was a weakling – it wasn't worth bringing up, so it was left to die!

BACKSTROKE?

Girls were named after eight days – boys on the ninth day. Girls would usually take their father's name – but change the "-us" on the end to "-a". So the daughter of Julius became Julia, the daughter of Claudius was Claudia, Flavius was the father of Flavia and so on.

Children would probably have "pet names" or nicknames. One girl was known as "Trifosa" – that means "delicious"!

The Celt names had their own meanings . . .
- Boudicca meant "Victory".
- Cartimandua meant "White Filly".
- Grata meant "Welcome".

Then, if you survived your birth and you could live with your name, you had to face the terrors of the rotten Roman schools . . .

Suffering schoolchildren – the good, the bad and the awful

Good: Schools cost parents money, so only the parents who could afford it sent their children. If you were poor you could miss going to school altogether.

Bad: Slave children didn't go to school. They were born slaves and belonged to the master.

Awful: Poor children missed school but had to work twice as hard for parents. If you didn't your parents might just decide to sell you! It was illegal to sell free children as slaves – but this didn't stop poor parents from doing it. There was not much chance of their being caught.

Good: Education was divided rather as it is today into primary, secondary and college.

Bad: Most children only went as far as primary.

Awful: For laziness in primary school you'd get the cane, or a beating if the teacher didn't have a cane handy. One poet described his bullying teacher like this . . .

His mouth's no good – but he has a hard fist. Why doesn't he become a boxer instead?

WHO ELSE FORGOT TO DO THEIR HOMEWORK?

Good: Primary schools usually had just 10–12 children.

Bad: That was not enough to pay a teacher's wage. So the poor teacher had another job – maybe in a workshop.

Awful: The Romans didn't have the figure zero. That made sums rottenly difficult to teach. Ask your teacher, "Can you add LXXXVIII and XII?" (The answer is "C")

Good: At least schoolchildren had their own goddess. Her name was Minerva. The holiday for the goddess was in March. After the holiday the school year began.

Bad: Each child had to provide their own wax tablets and stylus (sharp pen to scratch letters into the wax), their pen and ink, their paper rolls and abacus (counting frame).

Awful: For a serious offence in the secondary school – a flogging with a leather whip while other pupils held you down.

Good: Schools closed every ninth day for the market – it was probably too noisy to teach on market days.

Bad: Primary schools were pretty boring. You'd study mainly the three 'Rs' – reading, 'riting and 'rithmetic.

Awful: At secondary school you had to study mega-boring grammar and literature, with some geography and, of course, horrible history! By the time you got to college you had to study for public speaking – the Romans believed that good talkers made good leaders. (Do you agree?)

A grim life for girls

Through most periods of history it's been harder being a woman than being a man. It was no different in Roman Britain . . .

1 Roman girls were lucky . . . if they lived! "If you give birth to a boy, look after it – but if it is a girl then let it die!" (Letter from Hilarion to his wife.)

2 Men weren't happy with the idea of an educated woman. "I hate a woman who reads", wrote Juvenal in the 1st century AD.

3 Roman women had to be "controlled" from an early age. They were given a lucky charm at birth. Why? Because they didn't have a man of their own to protect them. When a baby girl was eight days old she was taken to a special ceremony. A gold or leather heart was hung around her neck. She would keep it throughout her childhood.

4 When a Roman girl was 14 she was ready for marriage. Who said so? Her father. A husband would be chosen for her. Who chose? Her father. What if the girl didn't like her father's choice? Bad luck. She'd have to marry him anyway.

5 On the evening before the wedding a special event took place. The girl placed all her toys and childhood clothes on the altar of the Lares – the household gods. She also took off her lucky charm – she had a husband to protect her now.

6 The bride always wore a white woollen tunic. It was held at the waist with a woollen belt tied in a special knot. She wore a bright yellow cloak and sandals. Her head was covered with a flame-coloured veil.

7 Roman women wore make-up. They used chalk to whiten their necks because a pale skin was supposed to be a sign of beauty.

8 If a woman's lips and cheeks weren't red enough then they would use a reddish earth called ochre.

9 Women were expected to remove hair from their legs as well as from under their arms. They rubbed hair off with a stone or used a cream to dissolve it – and it's a wonder the creams didn't dissolve the skin too! One hair-remover consisted of the blood of a wild she-goat mixed with sea-palm and powdered viper. Then, if you wanted to stop the hair growing back again, you would have to rub on the blood of a hare.

10 If a girl's eyebrows weren't dark enough then she might have used a metallic stuff called antimony. No antimony? Then girls used ashes! Imagine walking around with mud on your face, chalk on your neck and ashes on your eyebrows. If you got carried away you'd look more like a scarecrow.

77

Rotten Roman stories

The Romans knew some pretty rotten stories. Stories of gods, graves and guts. Their own gods were a bit boring. But then they heard the stories of the Greek gods. Those gods were much more like interesting people. So the Romans pinched the Greek legends and made them their own. Stories like that of Prometheus . . .

The Eagle has landed . . . again . . . and again . . . and again . . .

The fat, feathered fiend landed on the rock and looked at the man who lay chained to it. The bird's beak was as hooked as a hairpin. His great golden eyes glinted in the harsh sun. "Cor! Stone the crows! What a tasty sight!" he croaked. If he'd had lips he would have licked them. Instead he licked his beak.

The young prisoner lifted his head wearily. He was a handsome young man with nothing on but a loin cloth. He squinted through the fierce sun and glared at the bird. "Push off," he snapped.

The bird hopped from one hot foot to the other. "Hey! That's no way to speak to me! I'll have you know I'm an eagle – king of the birds!"

"Sorry, I'm sure," the man sneered. "I should have said, 'push off, your highness'."

The eagle shrugged. "No need to be offensive. I'm only doing my job. And a bird's gotta do what a bird's gotta do!"

"And I'm tired of every sparrow on Mount Olympus stopping off here to gawp and stare," the prisoner spat.

The bird breathed in deeply and ruffled its breast feathers importantly. "I am here on a mission. Some old geezer at the top of the mountain sent me."

"The *gods* live at the top of the mountain," the man said.

"Yeah, well some old *god* sent me, then. Big guy with long white hair and a bushy great beard."

"Zeus!"

"Bless you . . . anyway, he said, 'Fly down there and you'll see young Prometheus chained to a rock,'" the eagle went on.

"That's me! You've brought me the news that the great god Zeus has forgiven me? I'm to be set free?"

"Nah! The old guy told me to fly down here, and eat your liver."

HELLO LUNCH

"Eat my liver?" the young god groaned.

"Well, I didn't argue, did I?" the eagle chuckled. "I like a nice bit of fresh liver. Specially when its fried with a few onions."

"You'll kill me!" Prometheus cried.

"Nah! You're immortal. You'll 'liver' long time yet! Heh! Heh! Heh!" the bird cackled.

The god blinked as sweat ran into his eyes. "You'll hurt me," he sniffed.

"Can't be helped," the bird croaked and took a step towards his victim. "You must have done something pretty bad to deserve this!"

Prometheus sighed and looked towards the sun. "Once I could move through the air, just like you. One day I flew up to the sun itself. I brought its fire back down to earth."

"Good thing too – otherwise I'd have to eat your liver raw," the eagle chuckled nastily.

The young god went on, "I gave it to the humans to use."

"Sounds fair enough to me," the eagle admitted.

"Ah, but Zeus had told me *not* to give fire to the humans. He was furious. My punishment is to be chained to this mountainside.

"And to have your liver eaten," the eagle reminded him.

"Must you?" Prometheus groaned.

"Cor, stone the crows. You're supposed to be a hero, ain't you? Well, stop whingeing and let me get me dinner."

The bird lunged forward and Prometheus screamed.

When it was over the bird gripped the dripping liver in its talons and opened its wings. The mountain air lifted it gently off the mountainside and the eagle soared upwards. "See you tomorrow, Prommy!" it cried.

"Tomorrow!" Prometheus screamed. "What bit of me are you going to eat tomorrow?"

"Same again!" the eagle cawed. "That's the worst bit of the punishment. Your liver grows back. I'll come back tomorrow and eat it again . . . and the next day . . . and the next . . . until the end of time! Bye for now!"

Prometheus twisted his head to look at his side. There wasn't a mark to show the eagle's work.

And every day the eagle returned. Day after day,

month after month and year after year. Until one day . . .

"Hello there, Prom!" the eagle called happily as it clattered down onto the sun-warmed rock.

"Hello, Eddie," Prometheus grinned.

The eagle took a step back. "Er . . . you look happy this morning, Prom!"

The young god nodded happily. There was a gleam of pure nastiness in his eyes. Suddenly his hand shot forward and he grabbed the bird around its thick neck.

"Awk!" it squawked. "Your chains!"

"A friend of mine came along and snapped them for me," Prometheus smiled and his grip on the eagle's neck tightened. A huge man stepped from behind the rock. He had muscles that rippled like waves on the sea. "Meet Hercules. The greatest hero ever to walk the earth."

"Pleased to meet you, Herc!" the eagle gasped. "Er . . . if you'll just let me go, Prom, I'll get off back to me nest."

"You're going nowhere," Prometheus promised.

"Nah! I was getting sick of liver anyway," the big bird said weakly.

"Hercules is going to kill you," Prometheus said calmly.

"Look Prommy . . . mate . . . old pal . . . there was never anything *personal*, you know! I was only doing my *job!* Stone the crows, a bird's gotta do what a bird's gotta . . ."

His words were choked off with Prometheus' tight hand. He ignored the eagle's words. "But before I let Hercules kill you, guess what I'm going to do?"

"Er . . . me liver?" the bird guessed.

Prometheus nodded.

"Aw, no, Prommy. It'll taste really nasty – yeuch! Honest! Really sour."

"Ah, but you're forgetting one thing, Eddie. There's nothing in this world that tastes so sweet as . . . revenge!"

Did you know?
The founders of Rome, Romulus and Remus, were supposed to have survived being left to die on a hillside. A she-wolf adopted them. When they grew up, Romulus killed Remus and created Rome – named after Romulus, of course. If he hadn't, then this book might have been called, *The Rotten Remans!*

ROTTEN ROMAN FUN AND GAMES

Rotten Roman games

Which of the following modern games do you think the Romans had?

① HIDE-AND-SEEK

② TAG

③ COMPUTER GAMES

④ HOPSCOTCH

⑤ DOLLS WITH MOVING ARMS AND LEGS

⑥ LEAPFROG

⑦ KITES

⑧ BUILDING BLOCKS

⑨ SEE SAW

⑩ SWING

Answer: all except 3

Some Roman games you might like to try

Roman children's games were a bit like ours . . . only rottenly vicious at times!

Trigon

- Next time your parents slaughter a pig for dinner, ask them for the bladder – it's a part you won't be eating anyway.
- The bladder is cleaned out, then blown up like a balloon and tied.

- A triangle with sides about two metres long is drawn on the ground and a player stands at each corner of the triangle.
- The bladder-ball is passed from one player to another without it touching the ground.
- The aim of the game is to keep the bladder-ball in the air as long as possible.
- Easy? Then add two more balls so that each player has one. There is no set order for passing the ball. You may have to pass your ball while receiving two from the other players! (Game hint: It helps to have three hands.)
- If you drop a ball you lose a point. The winner is the one with the fewest drops in the time – say five minutes. (If you can't find a dead pig then use tennis balls.)

Knucklebones

- If your parents happen to sacrifice a sheep to the gods, ask if you can have one of its feet.
- Boil the sheep's foot until the flesh and skin fall away from the bones.
- Take the small, cubic bones and dry them. You now have five "chuck stones".
- Hold the bones in one hand. Throw them into the air. The aim is to see who can catch the most on the back of the hand.
  (Note: If your parents aren't sacrificing any sheep this week, you can use stones, dice or cubes of wood.)

Micare

- Play in pairs.
- Each player places their right hand behind their back.
- Agree on a signal – one player will nod, for example.
- On the signal, both players shoot out the right hand with a number of fingers raised.
- At the same moment each player calls out what they guess the total number of fingers will be.
- If neither guesses correctly then try again.
- The winner is the first one to guess correctly.
  (Note: This sounds easy. In fact, the more you play it, the more you learn to use clever tactics. Try it and see.)

The Jar Game
- Someone is selected to be "It".
- "It" sits on the ground – they are said to be "in the jar". The others try to prod or nip the one on the ground – rotten Roman children could be pretty vicious while playing this. (Warning! Only pinch or punch "It" if "It" happens to be a teacher.)
- The person in the jar cannot get up but they can try to grab hold of one of the touchers.
- The toucher who is grabbed goes into the jar.

Blind Man's Buff
- Someone is chosen to be blindfolded.
- The other players each have a stick and dance around tapping the "blind man" with the stick, shouting "Come and catch me!", which the blind-folded person tries to do.
- If a player is caught then the blindfolded person tries to guess who s/he is holding.
- If the blindfolded person is right then the caught player becomes the blindfolded one.

Nuts
- Each player has a supply of nuts – probably hazel nuts.
- Each player adds a nut to her/his pile to build a pyramid.
- The winner is the player who uses the most nuts before the pyramid collapses.
  (Note: This is a game for children. When you grew up the Romans would say you had "left your nuts". Perhaps you would like to ask your teacher, "When did you leave your nuts?")

86

Word games

If you like word-games or crosswords then you might like to make a "square" of words. They should read the same whether they are read from left to right or from top to bottom.

Here's an example from Reading in Roman Britain (now in Berkshire). It was found scratched on a tile . . .

Sator means "a sower".
Arepo is a man's name.
Tenet means "he holds".
Opera means "work" or "deeds".
Rotas means "wheels".
The square has also been translated as "The sower, Arepo, guides the wheels carefully."

BUT . . . some clever person worked out that this was not a word-game at all, but a secret, Christian prayer! Take all the letters and you can spell out the word PATERNOSTER. This is Latin for "Our Father" – the opening of the Lord's Prayer. There are two "A"s and two "O"s left over. These letters represent "the beginning and the end" to early Christians.

Clever, yes? But is it just coincidence? Or is it really a prayer? Make up your own mind.

Rotten grown-up games

The Romans enjoyed their circuses. But they weren't the sort of family day out we have at the circus today. No clowns, no jugglers, no tightrope walkers. But lots of violence, blood and death.

Augustine of Hippo wrote a book in which he told of his disgust at the bloodshed. His friend, Alypius, was taken to a Roman circus by some student friends. He set off for the circus, a real wimp. A band of trumpets played, bets were placed and the fighting began . . .

> *He shut his eyes tightly, determined to have nothing to do with these horrors. If only he had closed his ears as well! The fight drew a great roar from the crowd; this thrilled him so deeply that he could not contain his curiosity. When he saw the blood it was as though he had drunk a deep cup of savage passion. Instead of turning away he fixed his eyes upon the scene and drank in all its frenzy. He revelled in the wickedness of the fighting and was drunk with the fascination of the bloodshed.*

Julius Caesar, on the other hand, became a bit bored with the fighting and the dying. Long before the end of a contest he would begin reading reports and writing letters. This did *not* make him very popular with some of the spectators in the crowds!

SEEN ONE FIGHT TO THE DEATH, SEEN THEM ALL

BOO!

Gruesome gladiators – ten terrible truths

1 The Romans brought the gladiator fights to Britain ... battles between teams of armed men of whom half would be sure to lose their lives.

2 The idea of fighting and killing as a game probably began at funerals. The Roman Tertullian said ...

Once upon a time, people believed that the souls of the dead were kept happy with human blood, and so, at funerals, they sacrificed prisoners of war or slaves of poor quality.

DO I GET A SACRIFICE AT MY FUNERAL?

These sacrifices changed into fights to the death between two men at the funeral. They became so popular that they were taken away from the funeral and put in a huge arena. The fighters became known as gladiators.

3 In Rome there had been schools of gladiators, where a slave could train and fight for a gladiator master. If he won enough battles – and murdered enough opponents – he would win a fortune and his freedom. The greatest prize was the wooden sword – a symbol of freedom.

4 Nutty Nero even ordered a battle between a woman and a dwarf as a special spectacle.

5 When a victim fell in a battle an attendant would smack him on the head with a hammer to make sure he was dead.

6 If a fighter gave up, exhausted, he could surrender. The emperor would then decide if he deserved to live or not. The crowd would usually tell him by screaming, "*Mitte!* Let him go!" or, "*Iugula!* Kill him!" The emperor would signal his decision with his thumb. Thumb down for death – thumb up for life. And we still use that sign today.

DON'T MAKE ANY QUICK DECISIONS, MULL IT OVER A WHILE, THINK ABOUT IT, TAKE YOUR TIME

7 Some of the bloodiest battles were between criminals who were under sentence of death anyway. They fought till there was no one left – an unarmed man was put in the ring with an armed man who killed him. The armed man was then disarmed and the next man killed him. And so it went on – as soon as one victim fell, another was put in the ring.

8 There's not much evidence to show that the Romans in Britain brought the sort of wild animals to the arena that they brought to Rome itself.

9 There would be bears from Scotland which were chained to a post and tormented for the entertainment of the crowd.

10 Back in Rome they would have seen . . .

- elephants against armed men – until one day, the elephants crashed through iron railings and trampled the crowd. Caesar had a moat built round the arena to protect the spectators from the animals.
- sea battles in an arena which could be flooded to take warships.
- animals fighting each other to the death – bear against buffalo, buffalo against elephant, elephant against rhinoceros.
- crocodiles, giraffes, hippopotami and ostriches – the crocodiles were tricky because they didn't survive very well when taken out of Africa. One lot spoiled the fun by refusing to eat!

SLAVES SLAVES SLAVES, WHERE'S THE VARIETY?

- men against panthers, lions, leopards, tigers – but the men were usually heavily armed with spears, flaming torches, bows, lances and daggers. Some even took a pack of hounds into the arena to help them – they were in no more danger than the audience! One spectator made a joke about the emperor, Domitian. He was taken out of the crowd and thrown to a pack of dogs!
- men with cloaks against bulls – of the kind you can still see in Spain today.
- men fighting bears with their bare fists.
- five thousand beasts killed in one day of AD 80 in the Coliseum of Rome.

Amazing acts

But not every show in the arena was violent. Some of the acts used tame animals to perform tricks, rather as circus animals do today. The spectators were amused by . . .

- teams of tame panthers pulling chariots.
- a lion releasing a live hare from its mouth after it had caught it.
- a tiger licking the hand of its trainer.
- elephants kneeling in the sand in front of the emperor.
- elephants tracing Latin words in the sand with their trunks.

Petrifying plays

The Romans liked to visit the open-air theatres to watch plays. There were theatres in many of the bigger British towns. But if the plays were anything like the plays back in Rome, they would be banned today for being too violent!

The actors had real fights on stage. Then, Emperor Domitian allowed a real death on the stage. At the end of the play "Laureolis" the villain has to be crucified, tortured and torn apart by a bear. The actor playing the villain left the stage and his place was taken by a criminal who was under the sentence of death. The really rotten Romans enjoyed watching this horrible spectacle.

Then, of course, the Romans used the arenas as an excuse to execute people they didn't like – they put men, women and children in with wild animals, sometimes just for the simple crime of being Christians.

Strangely, it was the Christian religion that finally put an end to the massacres. When the emperors became Christian they banned the bloodthirsty events. On 1 October 326 AD, Emperor Constantine put a stop to the gladiator schools and, by the end of the century, the shows had disappeared from the empire.

Did you know?

The term "Roman Holiday" is still used to describe people enjoying themselves by watching others suffering. So, when teachers try to tell you the Romans "civilised" the Ancient Britons, you can tell them that the rotten Romans had some of the most "uncivilised" fun and games in history.

ROTTEN ROMAN FOOD

The Romans introduced new foods to Britain, and new recipes. They'd travelled the world and weren't too keen to eat the coarse bread or drink the ale of the Britons. They could afford spices to disguise the boring taste of the smoked or salted meat and fish.

Twenty foul food facts

1 The rich had great feasts. One Roman, called Trimalchio, held a feast which included wine that was a hundred years old. It also included a wild boar that, when sliced down the belly, allowed song-thrushes to fly out.

2 During such feasts the guests could eat so much that they had to be sick; a special room was set aside for them called a vomitorium. They would then go back into the dining room to continue eating!

3 Emperor Maximian was a big eater. He was supposed to have eaten 20 kilograms of meat a day ... that's about all the meat you'd get from a small sheep!

MUNCH MUNCH TWEET TWEET SCOFF SCOFF EAT EAT

4 Maximian also enjoyed about 34 litres of wine each day. Such gluttony killed him in the end, of course . . . but not until he'd reigned almost 20 years!

5 In the kitchen, the rich kept a special container used for fattening up their dormice. They were fed on the very best food – walnuts, acorns and chestnuts, before being killed, stuffed and served as a great delicacy. The stuffing could be made from pork sausage (or even sausage made from other dormice) and flavoured with pepper and nuts.

6 Snails fattened in milk were popular. Take your live snails out of their shells and put them in a shallow dish of milk and salt for a day. They love milk so they slurp it down, but the salt just makes the stupid creatures thirstier! Then they are placed in plain milk for a few days. They drink and drink till they become too fat to get back in their shells. Fried in oil and served covered in wine sauce – they are delicious!

7 Even fouler . . . fatten up the snails on raw flesh to add to their flavour. (Most snails would be vampire snails given the chance!)

8 The Romans enjoyed stuffed thrush. No worse than your Sunday chicken, right? Wrong! They stuffed the thrush through the throat without taking the insides out! Yeuch! The Romans also ate other birds that we wouldn't usually think of eating. They enjoyed . . .

- herring-gulls
- jackdaws
- crows
- ravens
- swans
- coots
- peacocks

9 The Romans didn't waste much. One recipe by Apicius calls for the chopped-up udder of a sow. They also ate the brains of animals . . . not to mention the lungs of goats and sheep.

10 King Mithradates of Pontus in Asia was scared of being poisoned, so he ate . . . poison! In small doses, of course. That way his body built up a resistance to poison. Then he heard the Romans were coming to get him and he hadn't the guts to face them. So he swallowed poison. Of course, it didn't work! He had to fall on his sword in the end. (So, when the Romans found him he had even less guts!)

THIS JUST ISN'T MY DAY

11 The Romans had some rotten drinks, too. One was made from the guts of fish. They were salted and left to rot in the sun. After a few days the liquid was drained off and drunk or used as a sauce – the way you may sprinkle tomato ketchup on your chips. (This may sound a fishy story, but it's true!)

12 The Romans ate chicken, duck and goose, just as we still do. But the Romans probably served them at the table with the heads cut off but the feet still on!

13 In Roman times there were storks living in Britain. The Romans ate those too. (Could you tell stork from mutton?)

14 Horse bones have been found at Verulamium, which shows that the Romans ate horse-meat sausages. (Neigh! It's true!)

15 For vegetables, the Romans used some pretty odd things. Would you have eaten a salad made with dandelion leaves? How about an egg custard made with nettles? Or perhaps you'd prefer some stewed seaweed? These things are still eaten today in various parts of the world.

16 Sometimes, Roman banquet guests would drop rose petals into their wine.

17 At one meal, Heliogabalus served his guests 600 ostrich brains.

18 He also served peas mixed with grains of gold, and lentils mixed with precious stones – perhaps they liked rich food!

19 A favourite game was to disguise food so that it looked like something it wasn't! At one feast, roast piglets turned out to be made of pastry. At another, a nest seemed to be filled with eggs – but the eggs were made of pastry and inside, the "yolks" were made of spiced garden-warbler meat.

20 You might enjoy a meal while watching television. But could you eat at a Roman feast with dancers and acrobats, jugglers and clowns rushing around? Or even a pair of gladiators trying to kill each other?

The rotten Romans' daily diet

The main meals of the day for the Romans in Britain were:

MENU

BREAKFAST
BREAD AND FRUIT

LUNCH (PRANDIUM)
COLD EGGS, FISH OR VEGETABLES

DINNER (CENA)
GUSTATIO – TASTY THINGS LIKE RADISHES OR ASPARAGUS AS A STARTER.
PRIMAE MENSALA – THE MAIN COURSE; CHICKEN OR HARE AND FISH AND VEGETABLE DISHES.
SECUNDAE MENSAE – SWEET COURSE, INCLUDING FRUIT

Rotten Roman beastly banquet

Why not invite your friends to a Roman-style banquet. Or, even better, invite your enemies.

First get your slaves to lay the table with napkins for each guest, a spoon and a knife. No forks, you will notice. If you want to try a Roman banquet then you'll have to eat with your fingers and have a napkin to keep your fingers clean! For the soft food and sauces you can use a spoon, and a knife for cutting or spearing meat.

Before you start, place some of your food in a small bowl in front of the statue of the family god. (If the god doesn't eat it then the slaves will!)

Say a few prayers. The Romans would say, "*Auguste, patri patriae*" – "Good luck to the emperor, father of our country."

Have your slaves wash and dry the feet of your guests. (If you can't find any slaves at the local supermarket or corner shop then you could always use a parent or teacher.)

Warning: Do not cook this food yourself! Have it done for you by your slaves!

Starter *(Gustatio)*

If your local shop doesn't have stuffed dormice or snails fattened in milk, then you may like to try shellfish, hard-boiled eggs or a dish of olives. Serve with spiced wine – or in your case, grape juice!

SPICED WINE

INGREDIENTS:
- I LITRE OF GRAPE JUICE
- 3 TABLESPOONS OF HONEY
- MIXED SPICE
- CINNAMON
- NUTMEG
- BLACK PEPPER
- WATER

METHOD:
- POUR GRAPE JUICE INTO A 2 LITRE SERVING JUG
- ADD A LITRE OF WATER – LESS IF YOU LIKE YOUR WINE STRONG
- STIR IN THE HONEY TILL IT DISSOLVES
- ADD A PINCH OF MIXED SPICE, ONE OF NUTMEG, CINNAMON AND BLACK PEPPER.
- TASTE IT AND ADD MORE HONEY IF IT'S NOT SWEET ENOUGH OR SPICES IF YOU WANT IT TASTIER.

NUMIDIAN CHICKEN

INGREDIENTS:
- CHICKEN PIECES (1 FOR EACH PERSON)
- CUMIN POWDER (QUARTER TEASPOON)
- CORIANDER SEEDS (QUARTER TEASPOON)
- 4 DATES (CHOPPED INTO SMALL PIECES)
- CHOPPED NUTS (4 TABLESPOONS)
- HONEY (2 TABLESPOONS)
- WINE VINEGAR (2 TABLESPOONS)
- CHICKEN STOCK (1 CHICKEN STOCK CUBE CRUMBLED IN A CUP OF WATER)
- PEPPER (A PINCH)
- COOKING OIL (1 TABLESPOON)
- BREAD CRUMBS (1 SLICE OF DRY BREAD)

METHOD:
- PUT THE CHICKEN PIECES IN A ROASTING DISH. BRUSH THEM WITH COOKING OIL, SPRINKLE THEM WITH PEPPER AND COVER THE DISH WITH COOKING FOIL. ROAST THE PIECES AT 350°F, 180°C OR GAS MARK 4 FOR HALF AN HOUR.
- WHILE THE CHICKEN IS ROASTING, PUT THE OTHER INGREDIENTS INTO A PAN AND SIMMER FOR TWENTY MINUTES TO MAKE NUMIDIAN SAUCE.
- WHEN THE CHICKEN PIECES ARE READY, PUT THEM ON A SERVING DISH AND POUR OVER THE SAUCE
- SERVE THE CHICKEN WITH VEGETABLES – CABBAGES AND BEANS ARE VERY ROMAN.

DATES COOKED IN HONEY

INGREDIENTS:
- 12 FRESH DATES*
- 12 HALF WALNUTS
- 4 TABLESPOONS HONEY
- SALT
- BLACK PEPPER

  (*IF YOU CAN'T GET FRESH DATES THEN A PACKET OF COOKING DATES WILL DO)

METHOD:
- PEEL THE DATES AND TAKE OUT THE STONES.
- REPLACE EACH STONE WITH A HALF WALNUT
- SPRINKLE EACH DATE LIGHTLY WITH SALT
- MELT THE HONEY IN A PAN AND GENTLY COOK THE DATES IN THE HONEY
- AFTER COOKING FOR FIVE MINUTES, TAKE OUT THE DATES AND ARRANGE ON A SERVING DISH
- SPOON MORE HONEY OVER THE HOT DATES
- SPRINKLE ON A LITTLE BLACK PEPPER AND SERVE

Finish off with fruit and nuts and grape-juice wine. While eating your meal, have some entertainment from jugglers, dancers, singers or musicians.

It isn't polite to talk too much at a Roman banquet. But if you must talk, then don't chatter about common things – football, fashion or the neighbour's new car – talk about important things like life, death and great teachers of our time.

Rotten Roman remedies

It didn't do to be sick in Roman times. Sometimes the cure was worse than the illness! Here's a letter from a Roman, Cassius, to his sister, Juliet. Would you like to try some of his cures . . .?

DEAREST JULIET

I HAVE BEEN VERY WORRIED EVER SINCE I GOT YOUR LETTER TELLING ME THAT YOR WERE BITTEN BY A SPIDER HIDDEN AMONG THE VEGETABLES FROM THE GARDEN. IN APULIA THERE ARE A LOT OF DANGEROUS SPIDERS CALLED TARANTULAS. THE BEST REMEDY FOR THEIR BITE IS, AS YOU KNOW, TO CRUSH THE BODY OF THE SPIDER ON THE WOUND. IF THAT IS IMPOSSIBLE THEN COVER THE SPOT WITH A PIECE OF ITS WEB.

ALTHOUGH YOU TELL ME YOU ARE BETTER I ADVISE YOU TO COME TO ROME AS SOON AS YOU CAN. WE WILL GO TOGETHER TO MAKE A SACRIFICE AT THE TEMPLE OF THE GODDESS CYBELE.

THERE ARE ALSO SOME USEFUL REMEDIES USING FROGS AS INGREDIENTS. A BROTH MADE OF SHRIMPS, FLOUR AND FROGS, BOILED IN WINE IS EXCELLENT FOR ANYONE WHO HAS LOST WEIGHT AND IS SUFFERING FROM TIREDNESS. CRUSHED FROGS, SOAKED IN WINE, ARE GOOD AGAINST THE POISONING OF TOADS.

FINALLY, TO CURE THE KIND OF FEVER WHICH COMES AROUND EVERY FOUR DAYS, YOU SHOULD EAT THE FLESH OF FROGS COOKED IN OLIVE OIL.

GIVE MY GREETINGS TO YOUR HUSBAND AND MY GOOD WISHES TO YOURSELF

YOUR LOVING BROTHER,

CASSIUS

ROTTEN ROMAN RELIGIONS

The Romans brought their religion and their gods with them from Rome, though in time they became mixed with the native British religions.

Lucky charms and cruel curses

In the Roman home the Lares were very important. These were household gods. They protected the home from evil spirits. In richer homes, Romans would also worship gods like . . .

Vesta – goddess of the fire and hearth . . . and you can still buy matches called "Vestas"!

Penates – guardian of the store cupboard . . . made sure nobody sneaked any midnight feasts.

Janus – the two-faced god who used his two faces to watch the people coming into the house and those going out.

The hot spring waters in the city of Bath are used as cures for all sorts of illnesses by people today. They were used by the Romans too. The Romans were a bit superstitious and believed there was magic in the water. They threw things into the water to take advantage of its powers. They threw coins in – probably as you would into a wishing well – 12,000 Roman coins have been found there.

They also threw in written tablets, usually trying to make a deal with a god – "You do this for me, god, and I'll build an altar for you, OK?" Many of these requests were for curses – if the name of the person you wanted to curse was written backwards, then the magic would be even stronger.

One man lost his girlfriend, Vilbia, to another man. He scratched the curse on a piece of metal . . . but wrote it backwards. Then he threw it in the water where it was found hundreds of years later. It read . . .

retaw ekil diuqil otni nrut ot em morf aibliV koot ohw nosrep eht tnaw I

(Do you know anyone you'd like to turn into a real drip?)

An even nastier curse has been found in Clothall. It was nailed onto some object, perhaps a dead animal, and says . . .

Tacita is cursed by this and will be decayed like rotting blood.

The waters of Bath weren't just used for cursing. The waters were famous for healing long before the Romans came to Britain . . .

The story of Bladud

BLADUD WAS THE SON OF A KING OF THE BRITONS

THAT'S MY LAD BLAD!

BUT BLADUD BECAME ILL WITH LEPROSY, HE HAD TO LEAVE HOME

THAT'S SAD BLAD

BYE... DAD

HIS MOTHER GAVE HIM A RING

COME BACK WHEN YOU'RE NOT SO BAD BLAD

HE LEFT AND FOUND A JOB AS A PIG KEEPER

I ONCE WORE ROBES BUT NOW I'M A POORLY CLAD BLAD

OINK

BUT TRAGEDY STRUCK! THE PIGS CAUGHT LEPROSY FROM BLAD!

WORST ITCH I'VE EVER HAD, BLAD!

THE ITCHING DROVE THE PIGS WILD, THEY RAN DOWN THE HILL AND INTO AN OOZING, BLACK BOG

I'M GOING MAD, BLAD!

Nasty native religions

1 The Celts believed that gods and spirits were present in all natural things.

2 Their priests were known as Druids. The Druids were local judges as well as priests. If they sentenced you to be kept out of the temple, then no one would want to speak to you.

3 Most of the religious ceremonies were held in woods – especially oak woods where there were magical mistletoe plants.

4 At first the Romans allowed the Celtic religion to continue alongside their own. They even allowed the Druids to build temples similar to the Roman ones.

5 After a while they began to suspect the Druids of leading the rebellions against Roman rule. Most of the Druids were put to death.

6 The Celtic heaven was like earth – only better! There was no old age or sickness and everyone was beautiful. The sun always shone, the birds always sang and there was always plenty to eat and drink. Food appeared as if by magic whenever you felt like it.

7 Death and heaven were so good that the warriors were quite keen to get there! That's why they were so fearless in battle . . . they didn't mind dying.

8 The one thing that the Celtic warrior feared was the sky falling down! That's what would happen if the gods were upset.

9 When you died, your soul went to heaven on a horse. Horses were very special to the British Celts.

10 Julius Caesar told a story of mass sacrifice carried out by the Celts. He said the priests had a huge man made out of wood and woven basket material. The giant, hollow man was then stuffed with living men, women and children . . . and set alight! Caesar could have been fibbing, of course, but the British Celts were great believers in giants . . .

The History of Britain . . . by a mad monk!

In the 12th century, Geoffrey of Monmouth told the story of Britain. It was not the history that you will read here and it's not the history your teachers will tell you! But we could be wrong and Geoffrey could be right. What do you think? Here's Geoffrey's history . . .

After the Trojan War – you know, the one where the siege of Troy was ended with the trick of the wooden horse – Brutus and his Trojan warriors came to Britain. Of course, the Trojan War was in the 13th century BC . . . before Rome was even thought of.

Brutus found that the British Isles were inhabited by giants. Brutus gave General Corineus the job of conquering Cornwall. Corineus killed the giants and was left with just one final giant – Gogmagog. Corineus wrestled with the four-metre man and threw him to his death in the sea. That's how Britain came to be free of giants!

Believe that, do you? Or is it just a TALL story? Old Geoffrey believed it. And so did many Britons, probably.

The Britons had their own stories and many were stories of heroes fighting giants. Some of the stories are still told today. But, because children are easily scared, most story-tellers miss out the gory bits.

Here's an old British folk-tale with the gory bits put back in. If you suffer from nightmares *don't read it* . . . or read it with your eyes shut. You have been warned!

A bloody British tale

Once upon a long-ago time in Cornwall, there lived the giant, Cormoran, with his wife, Cormelian.

Cormoran was big and Cormoran was a bully. "I want a castle and I want it built of white granite!" he told his wife.

"That'll be nice, dear," his wife nodded. "But there's no white granite round here. Only green granite. You'll have ever so far to carry it!"

"I won't carry it," Cormoran sneered. "You will!"

"Will I?" Cormelian blinked. "Why?"

"Because I'm telling you to," the cruel man cackled. "Now, get started!"

Cormelian trudged off to find the white granite and struggled to carry it back. Even though every step took her six miles it was hard and heavy work. When she returned the third time she saw that Cormoran was asleep.

"I'll just fetch a few loads of the green granite," the giant's wife sighed. "He'll never notice!"

But, as she brought the load of green stone. Cormoran woke up. "What's this?" he roared and gave her such a kick that her apron strings snapped. The stones tumbled down and sank Mount's Bay forest into the sea and drowned the people.

"Now look what you made me do!" Cormelian grumbled, rubbing her sore bum. She went off in a huff.

Cormoran piled the white granite into a castle – you can see it today in Cornwall. It's known as St Michael's Mount. The huge green stone that Cormelian dropped can be seen on the road to the mount.

Anyway, the poor people were horrified by the sinking of the forest. "Whatever shall we do?" they cried. "Mount's Bay forest has gone today – we'll be next!"

Just then, along came the local hero, Jack. Jack the giant-killer. Jack had killed giants by digging deep pits in the ground. When the giants fell in, their heads came up to the level of Jack. A quick whack with his axe would split the giants' skulls and kill them with a single blow. The pit became their gruesome, brain-spattered grave.

This time Jack had another plan.

First he collected as much food as he could find and placed it at the foot of St Michael's Mount.

Then he made a special coat with a huge pouch in the front.

Lastly he blew his horn to wake up the giant Cormoran. The angry giant glared at Jack. "What do you want, shorty?"

"I want to challenge you to an eating competition," the hero announced.

"No problem," the giant shrugged and sat down to stuff himself with a pile of food. Jack pretended to eat, but really slipped the food into the pouch in the front of his coat.

The giant began to slow down. At last he stopped. Jack nibbled at a roast cow. "Give in?" he asked cheerfully.

"Certainly not!" Cormoran roared. "But I'd like to know where you're putting all that food."

Jack shrugged. "In my stomach," he said, patting the front of his pouch. "In fact, I can empty my stomach and start again. Then I'm bound to win!"

"How?" the stupid giant asked.

Jack took a dagger from his belt. He placed it at one side of his pouch and dragged it across. The pouch split open and the food tumbled out. "Easy!"

"Hah! Two can play at that game," Cormoran sniffed. He took out his knife, stuck it in his fat belly and dragged it across. "Ouch!" he cried as the food tumbled out ... and most of his guts. "Ooooh!" he sobbed. "I think I've just killed meself!"

And he had.

A bloody end

An equally nasty story tells of the equally stupid giant, Bolster, who fell in love with the beautiful St Agnes. She asked him to prove his love by filling a hole in the ground with his blood. He agreed and opened a vein. He didn't know that the hole led to a cave that led out to the sea. Bolster bled for hours and died in the end. There's a hole at Chapel Porth in Cornwall, and red stains mark the rocks around!

The rottenest Roman religions

Chucking chickens

The Roman Army had its own religions and its own superstitions. The General of an army would look at the liver of certain animals for signs as to how a battle might go. They might also . . .

- observe the flight of birds – the ways in which crows flew, for example.
- observe the way the sacred chickens ate their food – Claudius Pulcher took chickens with him on a voyage to the Punic wars. The chickens were probably a bit seasick, because they refused to eat at all – a bad sign. So Claudius Pulcher ordered them to be thrown overboard with the words, "If they won't eat then let them drink!" He went on to lose the battle and the soldiers blamed him for drowning the sacred chickens!

Stomach signals

A Roman teacher, Fronto, wrote to his pupil, Marcus, with news that he had a pain in the stomach. He believed this was a sign from the gods that there was bad luck coming to his family. (If your teacher had a pain in the stomach, she'd be more likely to blame school dinners!)

Mighty Mithras

The religion of the bull-god Mithras, was very popular with many Roman soldiers. He was probably brought to Britain by the legionaries who served in Persia, where Mithras was a popular god.

Mithras was the "judge" of the afterlife – he decided who should go to heaven and who should go to hell after they died.

The temples of Mithras were dark and gloomy places – sometimes underground – and a lot of the soldiers must have enjoyed joining this religion, because it was like joining a secret society.

I CAN ONLY LET YOU IN ONCE YOU'VE TOLD ME THE SECRET PASSWORD, SHOWN ME YOUR SECRET RING, GIVEN ME THE SECRET HANDSHAKE, AND..ER..FOUND THE KEY

You couldn't enter the temples until you'd performed certain brave deeds – like allowing yourself to be locked up for several hours in a coffin! The base of the coffin was on the stone-cold floor and the side was close to a fire – you froze and fried at the same time!

Bull's blood

Another Eastern "mystery" religion had equally gruesome rituals, as Prudentius described in the 4th century AD . . .

The worshippers dig a deep pit and the High Priest is lowered into it. Above him they put a platform of loose planks. Each plank has tiny holes drilled in it. A huge bull is stood on the platform. They take a sacred hunting spear and drive it into the bull's heart. The hot blood spurts out of the deep wound. It falls through the holes in the planks like rotten rain onto the priest below. His clothes and body are covered in the animal's gore. Afterwards he climbs out of the pit. It is a dreadful sight to see.

Christianity

From the end of the first century AD, Christianity began to enter Britain. After the exciting Roman religions some Christians seemed a bit boring. One Christian writer, Tertullian, was against fancy clothes – he didn't even like to see them dyed. He wrote . . .

If God had wanted us to wear purple and sky-blue clothes, then He would have given us purple and sky-blue sheep!

PURPLE? WITH ALL THIS GREEN GRASS AROUND? WE'D CLASH!

By 250 AD, the emperors began stamping out Christianity and killing Christians. St Alban was one of the victims in Britain. Still, Christianity continued to grow there.

Then, in 313 AD, the Act of Toleration was passed that allowed Christians to worship openly. But it was all too late for poor old Alban . . .

The legend of St Alban

The wind blew wild and wet along the wall. Two soldiers shivered behind their shields and complained.

"End of the world, this place. End of the world!" old Laganus groaned.

"Not quite the end of the world," his young partner pointed out. "There are people on the other side of the wall!"

"People!" Laganus laughed. "Them Picts aren't *people!* More what you'd call *animals.* Proper people wouldn't live out in that wild country. They're *savages,* Paul, *savages!*"

Young Paul huddled into his cloak and looked across the bleak and empty moors. "Not as savage as the Romans can be," he said carefully.

"That's no way to talk about our masters!" Laganus gasped. "That's the sort of talk that'll get you beaten!"

Paul nodded. "That's what I mean. They'll beat me. They're cruel."

The older man snorted. "You're just soft, my boy. You've got to kill your enemy. Kill or get yourself killed. That's the way it is!"

"You wouldn't say that if you were a Christian," Paul told him.

Laganus turned on him savagely. "Yeh! I've heard

115

all about your Christian God! Look at that Alban!"

"They killed him!" Paul cried. "The Romans killed him!"

"But that's nothing to what your kind and gentle God did for revenge, is it?" the old soldier sneered. He sat down in the shelter of the wall and rubbed his freezing hands. "I heard the true story from a soldier of the Seventh Legion last week."

Paul crouched down beside him. "Alban was a hero. A Christian martyr . . ."

"Alban was a soldier just like you or me. Well, more like *you*, Paul. He was soft-hearted. Soft in the head too, if you ask me. The Romans were having one of their crackdowns on the Christians. You know the sort of thing. Killing a few here and there to show them who is boss."

"Murder," Paul muttered.

"Alban was a *Roman* soldier, of course. He should have been joining in the *killing* of the Christians. Instead he gave *shelter* to a Christian priest."

"Amphibalus," the young soldier nodded.

"And worse! He let this Amphibalus talk *him* into becoming a Christian!" Laganus groaned. "They sent soldiers to arrest Alban, of course. What did he do? Disguised himself and tried to run away."

"They caught him," Paul sighed.

"Of course they caught him! But they didn't kill him for hiding the enemy – they didn't kill him for becoming a Christian . . ."

"They did!" Paul cut in.

"No, no, no! They gave him a chance. They told him to make a sacrifice to the Roman gods. Prove that he was still loyal!" the old soldier said.

"He refused."

"So it serves him right if he was sentenced to

116

death," Laganus snorted. "But the Romans didn't have him tortured or crucified or stoned to death. No. They were kind. They sentenced him to a quick death by beheading!"

"They murdered him," Paul repeated stubbornly.

"Ah, but that was quick and kind. What happened at the execution, eh? You Christians never tell about that!"

The young soldier shrugged. "I don't know."

Laganus grinned. "Two soldiers led Alban to the place of execution. Alban managed to convert one of them on the way. But he didn't convert the second one, did he? The second executioner cut off Alban's head! *Then* your 'kind', kind God took his cruel, cruel revenge. As Alban's head hit the ground the executioner staggered back clutching his face. When the guards reached him they found that his eyes had both dropped out! Plop! Plop!"

By the end of that century, Christianity became the religion of the Roman State. But some parts of the British Isles were converted as the result of a strange accident . . .

Pirates, pagans and Patrick – Did you know?

1 Patrick is the patron saint of Ireland, BUT he was born in Wales, lived in England and his parents were Roman.

2 When he was 16 he was kidnapped by Celtic pirates and taken as a slave to Ireland.

3 He was given a rotten job by the Irish pagans. Looking after cattle on the bleak hills.

4 A boulder crashed down the mountainside towards Patrick. Just before it flattened him it split in two. One piece went on either side of him.

5 Patrick took this as a miracle. He believed it was a sign from God that there was special work for him.

6 He escaped to Gaul, then returned home to become a farmer. He still felt that his life had been saved for some special reason.

7 He boldly went back to Ireland.

8 He performed miracles there. There is a story, for example, that there are no snakes in Ireland because Patrick got rid of them all.

9 Patrick converted the kings of many Irish kingdoms to Christianity. The kings were baptised and the people followed the kings.

10 A king of southern Ireland had a rotten baptism. Patrick carried a crook – like a shepherd. It was pointed on the bottom. During the baptism Patrick accidentally put the point clean through the king's foot. The king didn't complain; he thought it was all part of the ceremony.

ROTTEN ROMAN FACTS

The rottenest Roman historian

At the eastern end of the Roman Wall is a fort. In 1971 the museum at the fort proudly showed their latest find. "It is a sestertius coin, made between 135 AD and 138 AD. On the back of the coin is a large letter 'R' – standing for Roma," they said.

Then an expert, Miss Fiona Gordon, told them they were wrong. The sestertius was, in fact, a free gift given away with bottles of fruit squash. "The letter 'R' stands for the name of the makers, Robinson!"

The museum keepers discovered Miss Gordon was correct. That was embarrassing! But, most embarrassing of all, Miss Fiona Gordon was just nine years old!

True or false?

1 A favourite method of execution in ancient Rome was "stinging to death".
2 The Roman Fort at Sinodum is supposed to be the site of a money-pit full of buried treasure.
3 Druids picked their victims by going "Eeny-meeny-miney-mo . . ."

REMIND ME, WHAT COMES AFTER MO?

4 Women could be Druids.

5 Druids would stab a victim in the back, then see the future from the way he died.

6 A crash at a chariot race was called "a plane-crash".

7 The Victorians pulled down the east end of Hadrian's Wall and used the stone to mend their roads.

8 The Romans didn't have peppermint toothpaste. They preferred powdered mouse-brains.

9 The Romans stopped traffic jams in Aldborough by building a bypass.

THIS ONE I'LL CALL A FLYOVER

10 In Roman horse races the losing horse was killed.

Answers:

1 True – the victim was smothered in honey then covered with angry wasps.

2 True – in the 19th century a local villager was digging at the fort one day when he came across an iron chest. A raven landed on it and said, "He is not born yet!" The villager thought this meant, "The person who can open the chest is not yet born." He filled the hole in and left. Are you the one born to open the chest?

3 True – according to Victorian experts. The shepherds of ancient Britain would count sheep with a number system that sounded very like "Eeny-meeny-miney-mo". The Druids could well have used it. Children may then have copied it as part of a gruesome game and it's been used in children's games ever since.

4 True – the Romans said that they met Druidesses. These women were good at telling fortunes.

5 True – the Roman historian, Strabo, said the way a man twisted and fell after he had been stabbed helped a Druid to read the fortunes for his tribe.

6 False – it was called a "shipwreck".

7 True. There are still large stretches of Hadrian's wall to be seen across the North of England. It's well looked after now . . . but it hasn't always been. Farmers pinched stones from the Wall to build their houses, and the Victorians were worse. They pulled the wall down, smashed up the stones into little bits and used them to repair the roads of Newcastle!

8 True – perhaps they wanted their teeth to be "squeaky" clean! They also used powdered horn, oyster-shell ash and the ashes of dogs' teeth mixed with honey.

9 True.

10 False – the *winning* horse was killed as a sacrifice to the god of war, Mars. The local people often fought fiercely to decide who would have the honour of sticking its head on their wall.

Rotten Roman towns

Everyone tells you about how marvellous the Roman baths were. But not *all* of the Romans were so keen. One Roman wrote . . .

> *I live above the public baths, and we all know what that means. Yeuch! It's sickening. Firstly there are the strong men doing exercises, swinging lead weights round with grunts and . . .*

SPLASH LA LA LA SLAP LA LA

CHATTER CHATTER GROAN ONE TWO ONE TWO SLAP SLAP

GRUNT OW!

... *groans. Then there are the lazy ones having a cheap massage – I can hear them being slapped on the back. Then there are the noises of fighters and thieves being arrested. Worst is the sound of the man who likes to hear his own voice in the bath. And what about the ones who leap into the bath and make a huge splash in the water?*

Rotten Romans today

The Rotten Romans ran the world for a long time. There are still signs of their life today.

Did you know?

1 The Romans signed their "trademark" wherever they went. They wrote the letters SPQR, which stood for Senatus Populus Que Romanus – The Senate and the People of Rome. The buses and the drain covers of Rome have the letters on them today.

2 The Roman language is called Latin. It is still used in some religious ceremonies and used to be taught in many schools. But no one speaks it as an everyday language now. So it's called a "dead" language. That's why schoolchildren who still have to learn it mutter the same old school chant . . .

LATIN IS A LANGUAGE
AS DEAD AS DEAD CAN BE
IT KILLED THE ANCIENT BRITONS –
AND NOW IT'S KILLING ME!

3 Much of the Roman Wall can still be seen – and walked along – in the north of England. But the famous historian and monk, St Bede, got his facts about Hadrian's wall completely wrong! He said the Romans built it just before they abandoned Britain. It was a sort of farewell present for the Britons, planned to keep the Picts and Scots out. He wrote . . .

> *When the Wall was finished, the Romans gave clear advice to the dejected Britons, then said goodbye to their friends and never returned. The gloomy British soldiers lived in terror day and night. Beyond the Wall the enemy constantly attacked them with hooked weapons, dragging the defenders down from the Wall and dashing them to the ground. At last the Britons abandoned their cities and the Wall and fled in confusion.*

Wrong! The Wall was there 300 years before the Romans left. Don't believe everything you read in history books – even if the writer is a saint!

4 There are some rotten things in Britain today that we can blame the Romans for. They brought them here. Things like . . .

- **stinging nettles** – next time you sit on one, you can cry out in agony, "Oooh! The rotten Romans!"
- **cabbages and peas** – the sort of vegetables your parents make you eat because "they're good for you." Next time you hear that, you can say, "The Ancient Britons survived a few million years without them!"

- **cats** – yes, blame the Romans for that mangy moggy that yowls all night on the corner of your street and keeps you awake. When teacher tells you off for yawning in class, say, "Don't blame me – blame the rotten Romans!"

5 Rotten spelling – a lot of the words we use today come from Latin. They made sense to the Rotten Romans but they don't make sense to us. Take the Latin word "plumbum".... no, it doesn't mean purple bottom. It means waterworks. So we get a word for a man who fixes your leaky waterworks from that. That's right, "plumber". We say it "plummer" and any sensible Briton in their right mind would spell it "plummer". But the Romans put that useless "b" in the middle, so we have to. Next time you get two out of ten for your spelling test say, "Don't blame me – blame the rotten Romans!"

6 False teeth – the Romans generally had good teeth. They cleaned them regularly and didn't have sugar to rot them. But, if they did lose a tooth, they used false teeth. These would be made of gold or ivory. They'd be held in place with gold wire. That wire could also be used to hold loose teeth in place. The poor people just had to let them drop out.

Ancient Roman Ancient Joke:

DOCTOR DOCTOR! HAVE YOU GOT SOMETHING TO KEEP MY TEETH IN?

CERTAINLY, MADAM, HERE'S A PAPER BAG!

7 Skyscrapers – the Romans made buildings with more floors than anyone else of their age. But this led to some rotten Roman tragedies. In 217 BC an ox escaped from the local market. It ran into a three-storey building and up the stairs. When it reached the top it threw itself out of a window on the top floor. By the time of Augustus the crowded cities were forcing people to build houses higher and higher – a bit like Britain in the 1960s! But many of these tower blocks began to collapse – so Augustus passed a law banning any building over 20 metres tall.

8 A family living in Hertford, England, are so keen on the Romans that they eat Roman food (like sardines stuffed with dates – yeuch!) and play Roman games after dinner. The family have organised a new Fourteenth Legion (but with only 24 legionaries so far) who go on 40-kilometre marches just as the original legion did. They also dress as Romans occasionally and go around schools to give demonstrations to children. This does not always have the desired result – sometimes younger pupils see the Roman soldier walk into the classroom and they burst into tears . . . usually the boys! Oh, and the daughter of the family isn't a fan of the Romans and is too embarrassed by her Roman family to bring her boyfriend home!

9 We have Christmas traditions today that live on from Roman times. One tradition is Roman and one British. They were . . .

- **holly** – The Romans had ceremonies for their god, Saturn, in December. The decoration they used was holly. Country people still believe that it's a protection against poison, storms, fire and "the evil eye".

- **mistletoe** – trees were sacred to the Britons. Mistletoe grew on trees and sucked the spirit from them – that's the sticky juice in the berries. The oak was the *most* sacred tree, so mistletoe from the oak was the most precious plant of all. Druids in white robes cut it with golden knives on the sixth day of a new moon. A sprig over the door protected the house from thunder, lightning and all evil.

OUR MISTLETOE MUST HAVE GONE OFF

10 Christianity put an end to the Druids' human sacrifices . . . but 2000 years later we may still have curious memories of those deadly days . . . the children's game *London Bridge is Falling Down*. Some form of this game is known all over the world.

Two children link hands and form an arch. The rest of the children have to pass under the arch while chanting the song. When a child is caught, then the bridge has fallen. That child becomes the "watchman" of the bridge.

But the legends say that, in the days of pagan beliefs, the unlucky child could only guard the bridge if he (or she) was dead! It seems the spirits of rivers hate bridges and without a sacrifice they would bring it down. The British legend says that children were sacrificed and their blood poured over the stones of the first London Bridge to keep "Old Father Thames" happy.

EPILOGUE

The Romans left to defend their homeland and Rome. The Britons were left to defend the island against enemies old and new. A historian from those times, Gildas, described how the "foul" Picts and Scots with their "lust for blood" swarmed over Hadrian's mighty Wall. They pulled the British defenders down from the Wall and killed them like "lambs are slaughtered by butchers". The men from the north with their hairy "hang-dog" faces took over.

Four hundred years before, the Britons had fought the Romans off. But in four hundred years the Britons had forgotten how to fight. Suddenly the Romans didn't seem so rotten after all. Now the Britons wrote and begged them to return . . .

The barbarians drive us to the sea, the sea drives us back to the barbarians. Between these two methods of death we are either massacred or drowned.

But no help came. Rome had problems of its own. After hundreds of years of Roman rule, Britain entered "The Dark Ages".

128